POLICE
RESEARCH AND
EVIDENCE-BASED
POLICING

THE PROFESSIONAL POLICING CURRICULUM IN PRACTICE

EMMA SPOONER, CRAIG HUGHES AND PHIL MIKE JONES
SERIES EDITOR: TONY BLOCKLEY

CRITICAL
PUBLISHING

First published in 2022 by Critical Publishing Ltd

All rights reserved. No part of this publication may be reproduced, stored in a retrieval system, or transmitted in any form or by any means, electronic, mechanical, photocopying, recording or otherwise, without prior permission in writing from the publisher.

The authors have made every effort to ensure the accuracy of information contained in this publication, but assume no responsibility for any errors, inaccuracies, inconsistencies and omissions. Likewise, every effort has been made to contact copyright holders. If any copyright material has been reproduced unwittingly and without permission the Publisher will gladly receive information enabling them to rectify any error or omission in subsequent editions.

Copyright © 2022 Emma Spooner, Craig Hughes and Phil Mike Jones

British Library Cataloguing in Publication Data
A CIP record for this book is available from the British Library

ISBN: 978-1-914171-86-4

This book is also available in the following e-book formats:
EPUB ISBN: 978-1-914171-87-1
Adobe e-book ISBN: 978-1-914171-88-8

The rights of Craig Hughes, Phil Mike Jones and Emma Spooner to be identified as the Authors of this work have been asserted by them in accordance with the Copyright, Design and Patents Act 1988.

Cover and text design by Out of House Limited
Project management by Newgen Publishing UK
Printed and bound in Great Britain by 4edge, Essex

To order, or for details of our bulk discounts, please go to our website www.criticalpublishing.com or contact our distributor, Ingram Publisher Services (IPS UK), 10 Thornbury Road, Plymouth PL6 7PP, telephone 01752 202301 or email IPSUK.orders@ingramcontent.com.

Critical Publishing
3 Connaught Road
St Albans
AL3 5RX

www.criticalpublishing.com

Printed on FSC
accredited paper

CONTENTS

ABOUT THE SERIES EDITOR

TONY BLOCKLEY

Tony Blockley is the Lead for Policing at Leeds Trinity University, responsible for co-ordinating policing higher education, including developing programmes and enhancing the current provision in line with the Police Education Qualifications Framework (PEQF) and supporting the College of Policing. He served within policing for over 30 years, including a role as Chief Superintendent and Head of Crime.

ABOUT THE AUTHORS

EMMA SPOONER

Emma is a lecturer at the University of Sunderland delivering work-based learning programmes to practitioners involved in investigative practice and policing. She draws on 21 years of policing experience as a front-line practitioner to help to de-mystify the research process and contextualise it into daily policing practice.

CRAIG HUGHES

Craig is Head of Policing at the University of Derby. He specialises in teaching financial and digital intelligence and investigation using evidence-based principles, drawing on 31 years of policing experience.

PHIL MIKE JONES

Phil is a senior lecturer in policing at the University of Derby, where he specialises in teaching research and study skills. He has over a decade of experience in research methods and has worked on research projects in the private, public, voluntary and higher education sectors.

FOREWORD

Police professionalism has seen significant developments over recent years, including the implementation of the Vision 2025 and the establishment of the Police Education Qualifications Framework (PEQF). There is no doubt that policing has become complex, and that complexity and associated challenges increase day by day with greater scrutiny, expectation and accountability. The educational component of police training and development therefore allows officers to gain a greater understanding and appreciation of the theories and activities associated with high-quality policing provision.

The scholastic element of the Vision 2025 provides an opportunity to engage in meaningful insight and debate around some of the most sensitive areas of policing while also taking the lessons of the past and utilising them to develop the service for the future. While there are many books and articles on numerous subjects associated with policing, this new series – *The Professional Policing Curriculum in Practice* – provides an insightful opportunity to start that journey. It distils the key concepts and topics within policing into an accessible format, combining theory and practice to provide you with a secure basis of knowledge and understanding.

Policing is now a degree-level entry profession, which has provided a unique opportunity to develop fully up-to-date books for student and trainee police officers that focus on the content of the PEQF curriculum, are tailored specifically to the new pre-join routes, and reflect the diversity and complexity of twenty-first-century society. Each book is stand-alone, but they also work together to layer information as you progress through your programme. The pedagogical features of the books have been carefully designed to improve your understanding and critical thinking skills within the context of policing. They include learning objectives, case studies, evidence-based practice examples, critical thinking and reflective activities, and summaries of key concepts. Each chapter also includes a guide to further reading, meaning you don't have to spend hours researching to find that piece of information you are looking for.

The concept of evidence-based policing is not new, and policing is fundamentally about being evidence based. This book shines a spotlight on the role of evidence-based policing in identifying opportunities and best practice to ensure policing is focused. It examines how the practice can be used as an investigative tool to identify and explore work-based issues and develop rational and supported conclusions to enhance practice.

The book discusses the key concepts in an understandable and relatable form, beginning with the management and analysis of existing literature and how to practically present the evidence obtained identifying best practice and lessons learnt. The reflective practice activities and the policing spotlights really demonstrate the principles of evidence-based research and its integration into UK policing.

Having been involved in policing for over 40 years, the benefits of these books are obvious to me: I see them becoming the go-to guides for the PEQF curriculum across all the various programmes associated with the framework, while also having relevance for more experienced officers.

Tony Blockley
Discipline Head: Policing
Leeds Trinity University

ACKNOWLEDGEMENTS

We owe a great deal of thanks to Sarah Turpie for her constructive feedback and suggestions that have helped make this book the best it can be.

Craig would also like to extend his thanks to his father-in-law Brian Cooke and his wife Sue Hughes for their constant support through the years.

Phil would like to thank his family – Hannah, Samuel and Ceci – for their kindness, support and endless patience.

Emma would like to thank her mum and dad and husband Ady for their belief, support and encouragement over many years.

CHAPTER 1
EVIDENCE-BASED POLICING

LEARNING OBJECTIVES

AFTER READING THIS CHAPTER YOU WILL BE ABLE TO:

- define what evidence-based policing is;

- describe why evidence-based policing is important;

- identify models to support the application of evidence-based policing;

- understand the risks of implementing new practice without an evidence base;

- explain how evidence-based practice can be applied in the criminal justice arena.

INTRODUCTION

Imagine the following scenario: you have a medical problem, such as a muscle pain, infection or minor mental illness. You use an online symptom checker service and it advises you to visit your doctor, so you book an appointment. You describe your symptoms to your doctor, who thinks about the problem for a moment before announcing that the best treatment for you is a course of bloodletting. What is your reaction? You may feel surprise, perhaps even horror, and promptly ask for a second opinion.

This scenario illustrates some of the key ideas that you will encounter in evidence-based policing. Here the intervention (treatment) that the doctor has prescribed was used up until the early twentieth century but is no longer considered good practice or a suitable therapy (except for a small number of specific illnesses). This is because evidence-based medicine has examined how effective bloodletting is at curing disease (the outcome we are interested in) and determined that it is not only ineffective but also harmful to patients (Greenstone, 2010).

Like doctors, as police officers your role in society is to reduce harm where possible. While a doctor reduces the harms of disease and illness, it is the role of the police to reduce the harms of crime. One of the interventions you might use is problem-oriented policing or hot spots policing, while a doctor might prescribe a course of antibiotics. Do you have a moral obligation as a police officer to provide the best-known treatment for crime, just as you hope your doctor offers you the best-known treatment for illness? Would you be happy to practise the policing equivalent of bloodletting? This illustrates why it is important to ensure practice is evidence-based and informed.

This is not just hypothetical. There have been real interventions that have been used in an attempt to reduce crime, reoffending and harm from crime that have not worked or even made things worse; some of these will be explored in this chapter as well as some that have provided benefits. The point is that it is important to check that what you are doing is actually helpful and not allow yourself to assume that what you are doing is automatically beneficial. Learning from mistakes is equally important as learning from success in evidence-based practice.

This chapter describes the key ideas outlined above. These include defining evidence-based policing, describing what counts as evidence, exploring what interventions are and how to measure outcomes. This is intended to raise your awareness of this important aspect of modern policing. The chapter concludes by introducing some recent evidence-based policing studies and their implications for policing practice.

DEFINING EVIDENCE-BASED POLICING

Sherman (1998, pp 3–4) was one of the early proponents of evidence-based policing. He defined it as:

> *the use of the best available research on the outcomes of police work to implement guidelines and evaluate agencies, units, and officers. Put more simply, evidence-based policing uses research to guide practice and evaluate practitioners. It uses the best evidence to shape the best practice.*

He describes two processes here.

1. Use evidence to underpin and develop practice.

2. Use evidence to evaluate the effectiveness of ongoing practices.

Developing these principles, the College of Policing has adopted a 'what works' approach incorporating evidence-based policing as the cornerstone of practice. Within this approach practitioners are encouraged to '*create, review and use the best available evidence to inform and challenge policies, practices and decisions*' (College of Policing, 2021g, p 1).

Evidence-based policing is about using research to support decision-making. Rather than merely collecting data and developing ideas or policies about how things *should* work, it is about bridging the divide and embedding that learning into practice. Evidence-based policing helps to ensure that the decisions you make and the actions you take have solid grounds: that you are not just acting on a best guess but are using *evidence* to guide and underpin your behaviours and practices.

One way of helping you to understand how evidence-based policing can support your practice is by considering the ATLAS model developed by the College of Policing (2016). Table 1.1 shows how you can apply the ATLAS model to help you generate questions about your practice.

Table 1.1 ATLAS approach to evidence-based policing

	Stage	What you may ask
A	**Ask** questions that challenge current practices	What are you doing?
		Why are you doing it?
		How could you do things better?
T	**Test** and critically evaluate existing research and innovative ideas	What does the current research say?
		How does it help you to understand your practice?
		How can you test new ideas to see what effect they have?
L	**Learn** from existing approaches and new ideas while considering how they work in workplace practices	What works and why?
		What is effective in the real world?
		How do existing approaches impact on practice?
A	**Adapt** practices and policies using the best available evidence	How can you influence practice?
		What needs to change?
		What evidence is there to support the proposed change?
		How can you implement the research?
S	**Share** the outcomes across the service	Who should know about your findings?
		How can you share the research?

(adapted from College of Policing, 2016)

By asking yourself these questions you are starting to think in an evidence-based way, moving beyond just accepting things as they are to trying to understand them and ensure they are as effective as possible. This can help to drive your own research into an area of practice. Research can be utilised to support evidence-based policing in two ways:

1. to develop a clearer or deeper understanding of an issue;

2. to evaluate the effectiveness of an intervention.

Therefore, you can create knowledge by developing a better understanding of your practice as well as drive change by trialling and assessing policing interventions, such as new policies or different working practices. These approaches will be explored throughout this chapter but first it is important to develop an understanding of what evidence is within an evidence-based policing approach and why this approach is important.

WHAT IS EVIDENCE?

The Oxford English Dictionary (2013) defines evidence as: '*Information indicating whether something is true or valid*'. It is the material that supports a particular position, view or idea. The material that can be used as evidence can be wide ranging and drawn from many different sources. However, not all evidence is equal; some types of evidence will be stronger than others. The stronger the evidence the more support there is for a particular notion. For example, a well-conducted systematic literature review that has examined a large number of papers, drawing together evidence from many studies, may be considered a stronger piece of evidence than a single report on a small-scale localised study. This does not mean that you should discard or ignore lower-level evidence but you will need to consider the relative strengths of the evidence you gather and examine. Chapter 2 explores the critical thinking skills that will support this process. Furthermore, Chapters 3, 4 and 5 discuss the relative strengths of different types of evidence as they are introduced throughout the rest of this book.

There are broadly speaking two ways that you will gather evidence. First, pre-existing evidence is what is already known and is available. You will be able to access and learn from it. To do this, you will draw on material, usually literature, that has already been produced. You will need to critically review this to ascertain how it relates to your own research project and how it helps to provide an evidence base for your own research. This type of evidence can be drawn from many different sources and Chapter 3 identifies some of the different places where you might find pre-existing evidence.

Second, there is evidence that you generate directly through your own research and by trialling, testing and evaluating interventions. However, your evidence needs to be reliable and valid, which requires utilising robust methods of collecting your data. You should follow recognised research approaches and be transparent in the processes you are undertaking. Chapter 5 explores how you can generate your own evidence in more depth.

You should recognise that this is the first step in your journey as an evidence-based researcher and that you will build your skills and experience over time. A project that gathers lower-level evidence that is well designed and carried out is much better than one which aims to gather higher-level evidence but is poorly constructed and conducted. In other words, do not try to take on too much for your first research project; you are unlikely to bring about a national change of policy from one piece of research conducted with limited time and resources. However, you can start to develop your skills and knowledge and begin to embed evidence-based policing into your daily practice. In this way, you will be able to support change as you grow and develop as both a researcher and a practitioner.

THE VALUE OF EVIDENCE-BASED POLICING

It is important that you view evidence-based policing as a practical tool rather than a theoretical academic exercise. The College of Policing (2020b, p 8) identifies that: '*Policing related research... will help us to improve police learning and development, and can directly inform practical, frontline policing*'. In this way, evidence-based policing adopts a pragmatic approach, looking at how research can support real-life policing issues in practice.

Policing needs to ensure it is as efficient and effective as possible given the resources and finances available. As society changes and new crime types emerge (for example, cyber-crime or artificial intelligence enabled crime), it is vital that policing adopts an effective approach based on evidence rather than a best guess. Even with long-held practices it can be healthy to review practices. Evidence-based policing allows you to challenge your own thinking and the normal accepted ways of working to test if they are still valid or if there is a better way of working.

Evidence-based policing encourages you to question and reflect on your practice, exploring what works and what does not work. It means learning from the successes as well as any failures. It encourages you to ask questions such as:

- do we really understand the problem?

- what impact is this approach having?

- are we being effective?

- why do we do things the way we do?

Policing should be adaptable, which means that it is necessary to challenge accepted practices in an appropriate manner to encourage innovation. Evidence-based policing develops problem-solving skills, critical thinking and analytical skills. It supports decision-making and develops professionals with a specialist knowledge base embedded in practice.

Kime and Wheller (2018) summarise the benefits of adopting an evidence-based policing approach as maximising the policing response for the public and minimising the risk of causing harm through policing practices. In this way, evidence-based policing supports practice for the individual practitioner, the organisation and wider society.

DECISION-MAKING: EXPERIENCE, ROUTINE AND HABIT

Evidence-based policing can support decision-making. This section considers the ways that it can do this by breaking out of traditional thinking patterns, habits and routines and moving beyond personal experience to using a wider evidence base. First, consider the following activity to reflect on what drives your practice at the moment.

REFLECTIVE PRACTICE 1.1

LEVEL 5

When Sherman (1998, p 6) was discussing the emergence of evidence-based policing he made the following observation:

> *Most police practice... is still shaped by local custom, opinions, theories, and subjective impressions.*

Analyse the above quote and answer the following questions.

- To what extent do you feel this is still true of policing practice today?

- To what extent do you base your own practice on either existing research, your training, your own experiences or observing what your colleagues do?

Sample answers to these questions are provided at the end of the book.

In reality, a combination of these is better than relying on any one method alone. Within policing one of the main ways you will learn is through observation of your colleagues. In the early stages of your career, this may be through a tutor and as you progress you are likely to learn from more experienced colleagues and supervisors. Observation allows you to identify how to behave in a situation; you may then adopt those practices and start to imitate them. In this way, learning through the social environment is key to police learning.

You will also undertake experiential learning, where you will learn from your own experiences. By doing this you are likely to adapt your practices and thinking based on your experiences.

You may also start to develop habits, routines and standard ways of working due to repeated exposure to similar experiences.

However, relying on observations and experience can be narrow. Consider the critical thinking exercise below.

CRITICAL THINKING ACTIVITY 1.1

LEVEL 4

Imagine a scenario where there has been a spate of robberies. It is your first day back at work after three rest days. Your sergeant asks you to develop a patrol strategy so she can target visible police presence to the maximum effect. You were working last weekend when several robberies took place in a suburb on the outskirts of the town at about 11pm. The crime analyst then emails you an analysis of all the robberies over the last month showing that 80 per cent of the robberies have been concentrated within a 200-metre radius of an underpass to the town centre. A total of 95 per cent of the robberies have occurred between 10pm and 1am but over the last three nights 75 per cent of the robberies have occurred between midnight and 1am.

a) Decide if you would base the patrol strategy on your own experience or on the analyst's product.

b) Compare the advantages of using the analyst's product to develop your patrol strategy to your own experience of where and when the robberies took place.

Sample answers to these questions are provided at the end of the book.

This is a simple example of how important it is to draw on a wider data set to ensure efficiency and effectiveness rather than relying on your own knowledge. Within evidence-based policing, this wider data set is often included in literature that reports the findings of other studies that have been conducted.

Your own individual experience is always going to be limited. You are only one person experiencing each situation. Even if you draw on the experiences of your colleagues on your team or within your station, this is still a small pocket of localised experience. However, your experiences can create mental maps of how to approach a problem. In this way you may develop well-worn tracks that you intuitively follow to guide your decision-making rather than drawing on the wider evidence base.

Additionally, within most organisations there is an organisational culture. This is sometimes described simply as 'a pattern of shared basic assumptions learned by a group [and] taught to new members as the correct way to perceive, think, and feel' (Schein, 2010, p 18). It is the informal working practices, routines and processes that have developed over time; it is the accepted way to think about and approach problems. When someone new joins an organisation, they are often socialised into that culture and the accepted way of thinking and behaving within that environment. This can lead to conformity and uniformity about the way to think and approach problems and ideas. In policing, because you learn directly from your colleagues, you are likely to have a similar outlook of how to approach a particular issue. Therefore, it is healthy to draw upon more diverse views to explore other possible approaches.

INTUITION OR EVIDENCE

Kahneman (2011) identifies that when making decisions, people employ either fast thinking, known as System 1, or slow thinking, known as System 2. System 1 thinking is intuitive and is very fast, automatic, impulsive and emotionally driven. Fast thinking is usually the first thing that comes to your mind. These decisions are cognitively easy as they are automatic, which will often lead you to follow your first impressions. Your instincts, habits, routines and normalised behaviours will all be expressed within this fast-thinking process.

System 2 thinking is slower and uses more analytical thinking to approach a problem; it is conscious and rational and takes more effort. In this system the decision-maker may consider different options and the advantages and disadvantages of those choices. It is slowed down and more deliberate thinking.

Each of these systems has a time and place to be used. While on patrol and faced with a time-critical incident you are likely to use System 1 thinking to make quick decisions, perhaps to preserve a life, prevent a crime or deal with an immediate problem. However, when you are faced with non-time-critical decision-making then it can be useful to employ System 2 thinking to slow down your thought processes and really explore the different options in a more systematic way.

Therefore, rather than relying only on your experience and quickly and intuitively assuming you know what will work, this approach encourages you to explore evidence to understand the issue in more depth. Understand why you may be thinking about things in a certain way and really subject them to deeper and slower consideration. This deeper understanding can then support your practice and help you to make more informed decisions when they are needed.

It is helpful to be aware of these processes because your decisions, and therefore your actions, can become embedded in routine, normalised and habitualised processes. This can be a barrier to innovation and change. As Sherman (2015, p 17) notes, '*evidence-based policing is about* adding *evidence to policing, not about* replacing *experience*'. Therefore, it should be seen as a blend between the craft and intuition of policing and the science of research; they should not be considered as mutually exclusive.

EVIDENCE-BASED POLICING APPROACHES

Earlier in the chapter it was identified that evidence-based policing (EBP) can help to develop a better understanding of an issue or to trial and evaluate an intervention. This section will explore how policing models can be used to support those dual purposes.

Within policing the SARA model is an approach adopted by problem-oriented policing (College of Policing, 2021b). Table 1.2 shows how it can be applied to help you approach an evidence-based project.

Table 1.2 The SARA model

Stage	What it means	How it supports EBP
Scanning	Identify problems and the consequences of those problems. Within this phase you may explore how frequently the problem is occurring and whether it is a long-term problem or a short-term one.	Understanding an issue
Analysis	Understand the factors impacting on this problem, identify what is already known about the problem and how it is currently being addressed. In this phase you also identify the relevant data that you need to collect to help you better understand the problem.	Understanding an issue
Response	In this phase you move on to identifying possible interventions, choosing an intervention and then implementing that intervention.	Trialling an intervention
Assessment	In this phase you need to evaluate the intervention, compare data gathered before and after the intervention, check to see if your goals have been achieved, identify any additional strategies required and importantly maintain an ongoing assessment to make sure the effectiveness of the measure continues.	Assessing an intervention

(adapted from ASU Center for Problem-Oriented Policing, 2021)

Evidence-based policing can be a method to help you understand your practice, identify where problems may be, and identify what works and why and what is not working and why.

Additionally, evidence-based policing is also about trialling and evaluating interventions. An intervention may be trial of a tactic, a new policy, a project, a piece of training, a new software package, a new piece of technology, a different way of working, new forms and so on. Think broadly when you think of interventions as they can include policies, procedures, projects and practices as well as trialling tactics and strategies.

APPLYING THE SARA MODEL

Within this section you will be able to see how the SARA model can be applied in a practical scenario.

POLICING SPOTLIGHT

Imagine a scenario where concerns have been raised as to whether victims of stalking are being correctly assessed for risk and therefore receiving the right level of support. From your own experience, you have noticed within your police station that investigators have difficulty completing the stalking risk assessment forms. You could use the SARA model in the following way to identify a number of potential different research projects (see Table 1.3).

Table 1.3 Application of SARA model to generate research projects

Stage	Possible evidence-based research projects	How it supports EBP
Scanning	You could consider a statistical analysis of completed forms to gather data on how many are completed (compared to how many cases are reported), how many are correctly filled out, how many are incomplete and how many contain the correct risk assessment profile. This may help to form an evidence base to support the argument that there is a problem rather than basing it on your own informal observations of what is happening.	Understanding an issue

⟶

Table 1.3 (*continued*)

Stage	Possible evidence-based research projects	How it supports EBP
Analysis	If previous research (or an HMICFRS or IOPC report perhaps) has identified that there is a problem with completion of stalking risk assessment forms, then you could undertake some research to explore why it is happening. You could consider interviewing police officers to explore their experiences of completing the risk assessments to try to identify some of the issues they face.	Understanding an issue
Response	If previous research has identified that police officers do not complete the forms correctly and they have reported that they have never received training, then you may consider developing an intervention. In this case you may trial a two-hour training event on stalking risk assessment completion.	Trialling an intervention
Assessment	This phase fits closely with the previous stage. Having conducted the trial of the new training you would then conduct an evaluation of it to see if it has made a difference. The trial and evaluation could form part of a single project.	Assessing an intervention
	Alternatively, you can conduct this phase on an intervention that you have not designed yourself. For example, in this scenario it may be that a new national training course has been introduced and you wish to conduct a research project to assess whether it is making a difference. In this instance you could consider comparing the products produced by officers that have undergone the training and those still waiting to complete it to assess any differences in performance.	

The important thing to take away from this is that you do not need to try to solve a whole problem in one go. You may have identified a problem but want to develop an evidence base to demonstrate the problem does exist and what its consequences are. This could be a project in itself, which could then provide the basis for further research at a later stage. Do not feel you need to go from identifying the problem, to evidencing it exists and solving it all in one project. Each phase can build upon the previous ones. As a brand-new researcher you may feel more comfortable in the scanning and analysis phases but do not feel daunted by the response and assessment phases. As you grow in knowledge, skills and experience, all of the phases are achievable for you as a researching practitioner.

TRIALLING AN INTERVENTION

If you are considering undertaking a research project that involves an intervention then you may consider using a logic model to help you plan, implement and evaluate the intervention (College of Policing, 2021c). The logic model and an example of how it can be applied using the stalking risk assessment example already outlined is shown in Table 1.4.

Table 1.4 Applying the logic model

Stage	Description	Application
Problem	Describe the problem; what does existing literature or data tell you about it?	Investigators are not accurately completing stalking risk assessment forms. Previous research with investigators has identified that they do not understand the relevance of some of the questions and do not feel confident completing the assessment.
Response	What are you planning to do? How do you think it will help to tackle the problem?	A training event is planned. This aims to raise awareness of the importance of the risk assessment and provide investigators with the confidence and tools to be able to ask the questions appropriately to victims to obtain accurate information.
Outputs	What will be produced following implementation of the response? This should be measurable, eg development of a new policy, number of people trained etc	All uniform police officers within one district who conduct stalking assessments as part of their role will complete the training package.
Outcomes	What changes do you anticipate as a result of the intervention? Think about short term, medium term and long term. How could you measure the impact of the intervention?	An increase in the number of correctly completed forms. Increase in investigators' knowledge of the rationale for the questions and confidence in completing the forms. The recorded risk levels could also be examined to analyse whether the additional training has helped officers to identify the level of risk more accurately.

You can use this model to help focus your research and any intervention that you plan to conduct.

MEASURING EFFECTIVENESS

When trialling an intervention, a key part of evidence-based practice is evaluating it to measure its effectiveness. The EMMIE model can help you to consider some of the key areas that you should consider as part of your evaluation (Johnson et al, 2015). Table 1.5 gives some examples of the types of questions you may want to ask.

Table 1.5 Evaluation using the EMMIE model

Stage	Questions to consider
Effect	Was the intervention effective or not? What effect did the intervention have? Did it achieve the outcomes?
Mechanism	How did the intervention actually work? What was it about the actual intervention that made it effective?
Moderator	What factors impact on its effectiveness? Does it work in some locations but not others? Does it work differently when applied at different times?
Implementation	How was the intervention implemented? Were there any practical issues with the implementation? Was it implemented in the way it had been planned?
Economic cost	How much did the intervention cost? What are the economic benefits of the intervention? Remember though that it is not always possible to put a monetary value on an intervention.

Each stage is measured to assess the overall strength of evidence. You can apply this model to your own evaluation of an intervention, or you can use this to help you critically evaluate studies that others have undertaken. You will see this model used throughout the College of Policing *What Works* website to evaluate studies and interventions.

NEED FOR ONGOING EVALUATION

While it is important to evaluate an intervention at the end of any trial period, it is just as important to maintain regular evaluations to ensure continuing effectiveness over time. Consider the following example that highlights the importance of this issue.

EVIDENCE-BASED POLICING

SEX OFFENDER TREATMENT PROGRAMME

The Core Sex Offender Treatment Programme (SOTP) was introduced in 1992 as a cognitive-behavioural group work programme for sex offenders who had been imprisoned. The programme underwent a number of amendments since its inception as the evidence base emerged. In 2017 a further evaluation was undertaken and found that there was little or no difference in the rates of reoffending between those that had completed SOTP and those that had not (Mews et al, 2017). In fact, in some cases there was evidence of a small increase in offending rates instead. Following the review, the Ministry of Justice ended the SOTP and replaced it with two new programmes.

This demonstrates the importance of maintaining an ongoing evaluation. Practices that worked once may not always work. Small incremental changes introduced over a long period of time may impact the overall effectiveness of any intervention; therefore, it is important to not just introduce something and then leave it. The need for ongoing monitoring and evaluation is a key part of evidence-based practice.

RISKS OF IMPLEMENTING AN INTERVENTION WITHOUT EVIDENCE

The importance of planning, conducting and evaluating interventions has been explored throughout this chapter. Interventions should draw on existing evidence to support their introduction rather than being based just on your own experiences, thoughts or opinions. You should have an idea of what the impact may be before you implement an intervention. To do this you should learn from the experiences of others and draw on previous research. Otherwise you risk wasting time and resources and potentially increasing risk due to ill-thought-out practice. Consider the following example and how research supports the decision-making.

POLICING SPOTLIGHT

SCARED STRAIGHT

Imagine you are working as part of a multi-disciplinary team looking at discouraging at-risk teenagers from becoming involved in crime. One of your colleagues says that they have heard of a programme called Scared Straight, where young people conduct supervised visits to prisons to speak to prisoners about their experiences and how they became involved in crime. It is intended as a deterrent to scare young people away from crime.

You can see some merits in this approach as a short sharp shock but you also have some reservations and are unsure of how it works in practice. You therefore choose to conduct some research to find out more about the programme. You locate the results of a systematic review of the Scared Straight programmes that was conducted by the College of Policing (2015). The review revealed that there is little to support the introduction of this initiative and in fact there is some evidence that the programmes actually increase crime rather than prevent it.

Based on this knowledge, your advice to the multi-disciplinary team is to not implement this intervention but to continue to explore other possible options.

Perhaps you can see from this example that it is more impactive to use the evidence to support your advice and decision rather than relying on your own opinion. Now you can try putting this into practice yourself in critical thinking activity 1.2.

CRITICAL THINKING ACTIVITY 1.2

LEVEL 6

Imagine there has been an increase in burglaries overnight on one of the estates in a suburb of your local town. Your colleague has suggested using a drone to conduct patrols as it has a single operator and can therefore save valuable resources. Evaluate this problem and the suggested solution by answering the following questions.

a) What do you anticipate achieving by using the drone (consider what outcomes you want)?

b) What do you think are the main legal and procedural issues in using the drone?

c) What else might you need to consider for using a drone to tackle burglary?

Sample answers to these questions are provided at the end of the book.

This should start to demonstrate how much you need to consider when undertaking evidence-based policing. However, taking the time to plan properly before trialling an intervention should make the actual trial and evaluation a more productive experience and truly add to the evidence base while minimising risk.

APPLICATIONS OF EVIDENCE-BASED PRACTICE TO THE CRIMINAL JUSTICE ARENA

The College of Policing website has two areas that may be of interest to you to explore how evidence-based practice is being applied.

1. A research map which lists research being conducted by practitioners throughout the country (College of Policing, 2021d). This shows the breadth of the research that is being undertaken.

2. Published research projects (College of Policing, 2021e). Within this section you will find a number of studies that have been undertaken by the College of Policing to help inform practitioners and add to the growing knowledge base of *what works*. Within this you will find systematic literature reviews, rapid evidence assessments and also evaluations of policing interventions.

You will find a wide range of evidence-based practice here and a few examples are outlined in the rest of this section to show the breadth of research available.

In an effort to streamline guidance and bring all best practice into one place, the College of Policing (2018) launched Authorised Professional Practice (APP) in 2013, an online database containing up-to-date guidance and doctrine. This incorporates a move to evidence-based policing with an underpinning theoretical or agreed practitioner foundation for all practice guidance. This is a significant ongoing project. One of the early pieces of research for APP was to develop evidence-based guidance for the initial contact with a victim or witness (College of Policing, 2021f). This draws together practitioner experience and research to make evidence-based recommendations on the best ways to obtain accurate and reliable information during the initial contact. This project developed practitioner-level guidance, strategic-level recommendations and suggestions for further research.

Evidence-based practice has also been instrumental in a wide variety of other areas, including the introduction of polygraph testing for some sex offenders and also the trial of polygraph testing for perpetrators of domestic abuse in certain high-risk situations (HM Government, 2021). Evidence-based evaluations are also being carried out on high-level policing changes such as direct entry superintendents, direct entry inspectors, fast-track inspectors, and the introduction of the Police Constable Degree Apprenticeship (see College of Policing, 2021e to access these reports).

This provides you with an idea of the scope of evidence-based policing and the potential applications for it. Hopefully, it inspires you to consider your own practice and how you may be able to contribute to the growing body of evidence-based practice.

SUMMARY OF KEY CONCEPTS

This chapter has discussed some of the following key concepts.

⚙ **Evidence-based policing:** make use of evidence to support and develop practice and to evaluate the effectiveness of policing interventions.

⚙ **What evidence is:** this can be wide ranging but it is material that supports an idea or a notion. It can be existing evidence that is already available or evidence that you generate through your own research.

⚙ **Importance of evidence-based policing:** it helps you to move away from your own experiences, subjective opinions and ideas and instead uses evidence to support decision-making.

⚙ **Models for measuring effectiveness:** the SARA model can help you to structure evidence-based research within a problem that you identify. If you wish to trial an intervention then the logic model can help you to plan, implement and evaluate it. Furthermore, the EMMIE model can support you with conducting an evaluation that is broader than just considering the effect of an intervention.

⚙ **Applications of evidence-based policing:** these are broad and are increasing. The College of Policing website provides a good starting place for exploring the applications of evidence-based policing and how it is utilised to support everyday policing.

CHECK YOUR KNOWLEDGE

1. How can evidence-based policing support your practice?

2. Why is it important to use evidence to support decision-making?

3. What are the dangers of introducing an intervention without establishing if there is an evidence base first?

4. Identify two pieces of evidence-based research that have been published on the College of Policing website.

FURTHER READING

ARTICLES IN JOURNALS

Dawson, P and Stanko, E A (2016) The Best-kept Secret(s) of Evidence Based Policing. *Legal Information Management*, 16(2): 64–71.
The above is an article that will help you to think about the range of data that is already collected by police organisations and may be utilised to support evidence-based policing.

The *Cambridge Journal of Evidence-based Policing* is an excellent resource to access contemporary research.

WEBSITES

College of Policing (2021) What Works Network. [online] Available at: https://whatworks.college.police.uk/Pages/default.aspx (accessed 15 January 2022).
The College of Policing 'What Works Network' is an important resource for you.

Society of Evidence Based Policing (2021) [online] Available at: www.sebp.police.uk (accessed 15 January 2022).
The Society of Evidence Based Policing is also an excellent resource to support your work as an evidence-based practitioner.

CHAPTER 2
RESEARCH AS AN INVESTIGATION

LEARNING OBJECTIVES

AFTER READING THIS CHAPTER YOU WILL BE ABLE TO:

✦ identify the similarities between an investigation and evidence-based research;

✦ describe why critical thinking skills are necessary for evidence-based research;

✦ explain how bias can impact on a research project;

✦ explain how to adopt a systematic approach to research;

✦ compare the skills required to conduct investigations and evidence-based research.

INTRODUCTION

As a new student to evidence-based research you may be feeling overwhelmed at what is expected of you. It can be daunting working out where to start, how to research a problem, how to gather and analyse information and how to use it to make evidence-based decisions and recommendations. This book is aimed at policing students and many of you reading it will either be working in the criminal justice arena or aspire to work within that field. Therefore, this chapter aims to contextualise the evidence-based research process and help you to understand it as an investigative practice. The following policing spotlight feature introduces you to some of these similarities.

POLICING SPOTLIGHT

A police officer receives a report that a man is selling drugs from his house. The officer checks the police databases for any information on the address and sees that a man lives there who has previous convictions for supplying drugs. The officer speaks to colleagues to see what they have done in similar circumstances and as a result arranges for surveillance on the house. The surveillance reveals a number of known drug users visiting the address. A search warrant is obtained, and some drugs are found along with a large sum of money. The man who lives there is arrested and charged with supplying drugs. A few weeks later the police officer phones the member of the public who had reported it, who confirms that there has been no further suspicious activity since the police intervened.

By following this course of action, the police officer is undertaking an investigation. She is identifying a problem, gathering information from different sources, taking action to help address the problem and then checking to see what impact the actions have had on the problem. This is the same process that you will follow when you conduct evidence-based research.

Viewing evidence-based research as an investigation can help to de-mystify the process. This chapter draws on the work-based process of investigation and compares it to evidence-based research to emphasise the similarities between them. It explores the investigative mindset required in policing and how this is linked to the development of critical thinking skills needed for evidence-based research. It demonstrates how evidence-based research adopts structured and systematic processes to information gathering in line with investigative practice and provides an introduction to evaluating and using that evidence. Finally, it highlights the transferrable skills between workplace investigative practice and evidence-based research.

RESEARCH AS AN INVESTIGATION

This section explores the similarities between an *investigation* and the *research* process. It begins with a critical thinking activity exploring these two terms.

CRITICAL THINKING ACTIVITY 2.1

LEVEL 4

In order to understand how research can be viewed as an investigation, it is first important to define what an investigation is and also to define what research is.

a) Write at least five words (or phrases) that define an investigation.

b) Write at least five words (or phrases) that define research.

Consider using a dictionary or thesaurus on your computer to help you with this task.

Sample answers to these questions are provided at the end of the book.

DEFINING RESEARCH AS AN INVESTIGATION

As you completed the previous activity you may have noticed duplication or similarity in the words you used to describe these two terms. If so, then you are starting to see the links between investigative practice and the research process. Oxford Dictionaries (2013) defines an investigation as: 'a systematic *inquiry into something so as to* establish the truth; *research into a subject*'. It goes on to define research as: 'the systematic *investigation into and study of material and sources in order to* establish facts *and reach new conclusions*'.

These definitions highlight the importance of adopting a systematic process. This means that your approach should be ordered and logical. You need to invest time in planning and have a clear focus for what you want to achieve. You should collect your evidence in a methodical manner and analyse and present it in a structured way.

Both definitions also refer to establishing facts or establishing the truth. Within evidence-based research this is about looking for the *best available evidence* to allow you to make informed decisions. As you work through this book you are encouraged to think about different types of information, how you assess it to determine what is the best available evidence, and how you can use it to support evidence-based policing.

INVESTIGATIVE RESEARCH SKILLS

In order to be an effective researcher, it is therefore important to possess good investigative skills. The College of Policing (2020b) identifies a number of areas that investigators need to be skilled in, including:

- applying the investigative mindset;

- planning;

- evaluating material to determine its value to an investigation.

These are also core skills for the researcher that are incorporated in the key concepts of *critical thinking*, *systematic examination* and *evidential evaluation*. These concepts are explored in more depth throughout the rest of the chapter.

CRITICAL THINKING SKILLS

One of the key similarities between work-based investigations and evidence-based research is the mindset that needs to be adopted. Policing has long adopted a mantra known as the ABC of investigation (College of Policing, 2019a).

- Assume nothing.

- Believe nobody.

- Challenge everything.

It is a critical approach where information is not accepted at face value and a questioning mindset is maintained. As an investigator you should adopt a neutral position and objectively assess the information. As a researcher this is also key to your studies. It is the ability to look beyond what you are reading, question what it is saying, assess how it fits in with everything else you know and truly understand the material.

Within academic research you will often see this referred to as *critical thinking*. It is a skill that you need to practise, develop and demonstrate within your research. Within policing, critical thinking is referred to as an *investigative mindset*; understanding this term can help you to see how it can be applied to evidence-based research.

INVESTIGATIVE MINDSET

An investigative mindset is defined as '*a state of mind or attitude which investigators adopt and which can be developed over time through continued use*' (ACPO and NPIA, 2012, p 84). There are five identified stages to demonstrating an investigative mindset (see Table 2.1).

Table 2.1 Investigative mindset

Stage	What it means	What you may ask yourself
Planning and preparation	Set an overall direction, identify key questions, and develop a plan to locate and gather relevant material. At this stage you may also start to develop theories or hypotheses that you want to test.	• What am I trying to achieve? • How can I achieve it? • What material is likely to be relevant to help me reach my objectives? • Where can I obtain information from? • How can I gather information and material?
Understanding your material	Understanding the origin of your material helps you to assess how reliable and valid it is.	• What is it? • Where has it come from? • Who has it come from? • When was it produced? • How was it produced?
Examination	Systematically collect and examine material; be thorough and pay attention to detail. Interpret it in relation to the bigger picture to help you understand how it all fits together.	• Are there any gaps? • Are there any inconsistencies? • Does this help me to understand what is happening?

→

Table 2.1 (continued)

Stage	What it means	What you may ask yourself
Recording and collating	Keep records and manage material that is gathered in order to support a structured approach and to display your processes.	• How can I demonstrate what I have done? • How can I protect the integrity of the material I have obtained?
Evaluating	Assess the material you have gathered to determine how it contributes to understanding or resolving the issues that have been identified.	• Have I achieved my aim? • Is the information gathered relevant? • Does it help me to understand the problem better? • Are there still gaps?

Within Table 2.1 you may be starting to see the similarities with the types of questions you could ask when conducting evidence-based research. It is the curious and questioning mindset that needs to be adopted.

The need for 'healthy scepticism' and 'respectful uncertainty' have been identified as important skills for investigators (Laming, 2003). Healthy scepticism means keeping an open mind and not accepting information unquestioningly. Respectful uncertainty means critically evaluating information. This is not a position of disbelief but rather one of inquisitiveness. Adopting a position of uncertainty allows you to keep questioning and seeking more information and drives you to try to establish the best available evidence.

CRITICAL THINKING

As you developed an understanding of the investigative mindset you may have been able to see how these skills could also be applied to demonstrate *critical thinking* within evidence-based research. There is a great deal of overlap and similarity. This is because research is an investigative process that encourages you to be curious. The questioning mindset and the impartial and objective approach is the same across both disciplines.

It is important to recognise that critical thinking, and being critical within the research process, is not about criticising. It is not looking for the fault in what you are reading. Rather it is about approaching the literature and the research process with an open and questioning mind. To do this you need to be reading actively rather than passively. This means that rather than merely reading and absorbing information unquestioningly you need to be thinking about what the information means. Keep asking questions such as:

• why is the author making this point?

• is there evidence to support what is being said?

• how does the material relate to other material you have read?

This conscious processing of information is an active thinking skill that you need to develop through practice. To help you with this when you are reading material, do not merely copy or just highlight lines of text. Instead, actively think about what you have read and try to summarise it in your own words, draw out the meaning of it and identify the questions that it raises and the thoughts that you have. This can feel exhausting at times, but it can help you to develop your critical thinking skills.

To help you to adopt a critical mindset it can be useful to use the 5WH rule of questioning:

• who?

• what?

• why?

• where?

• when?

• how?

Now apply this rule of questioning in the following critical thinking activity.

CRITICAL THINKING ACTIVITY 2.2

LEVEL 5

Consider the following fictional radio news broadcast: *Burglaries are at their highest rate for 15 years. The number of burglaries has increased by 50 per cent over the last 12 months. Local councillor Nicky Seville said: 'This is an awful situation for the*

$\longrightarrow$

hard-working citizens of our town; this is a result of the government policies where we have seen a huge reduction in police officers. We need the police back on the streets, visible to the public, catching criminals in the act and fighting this crime wave.'

Think critically about this news report and the issues it raises. To do this write out six questions you might ask yourself about the news report, the problem that has been identified and the proposed solution, using the 5WH words to start each question.

a) Who...

b) What...

c) Why...

d) Where...

e) When...

f) How...

Sample answers to these questions are provided at the end of the book.

When you are reviewing information that you have gathered for your research, these are the types of questions that you should keep asking yourself. Adopting these critical thinking skills should help you to demonstrate that you are moving beyond merely repeating what others are saying but you are actually understanding it and its relevance to your own research area.

RECOGNISING BIAS

One of the key skills in demonstrating critical thinking is the ability to remain open minded. This means being open to new ideas and different ways of thinking, being prepared to change your mind and to challenge what you think you know. You should adopt an unbiased approach to the material you are examining.

The search for the best available evidence means that you need to remain impartial. The Ministry of Justice (2020, p 6) stress that investigators should *pursue all reasonable lines of inquiry; whether these point towards and away from a suspect*'. This is to ensure a fair and balanced investigation. It is telling the investigator that they should not be biased one way or the other. If a police officer arrested and interviewed a suspect and he said that he had an alibi for the time of the offence, would you expect the police officer to explore that alibi? Hopefully you would, because you should expect the police will conduct a balanced enquiry and not just look at one side of the evidence. This is the impartial nature of being an investigator.

The need for impartiality is equally true of the research process. You may have a preconceived idea of what you think about a particular subject you are researching but you need to explore it from different angles. The following reflective thinking activity encourages you to start thinking beyond your initial thoughts and adopting a wider view on the research topic. As you complete this exercise pay attention to your initial instinctive thoughts and then reflect more deeply about those responses.

REFLECTIVE PRACTICE 2.1

LEVEL 5

Your sergeant is considering how to increase police officers' time on visible patrol. One method the sergeant has suggested is to encourage all police officers to take their refreshment breaks in public in their local patrol area.

- What are your initial thoughts on this proposal?

- Do you think this is a good idea or a bad idea and why?

- Now think about this from these different perspectives:

  o members of the public;

  o the police organisation;

  o the individual officers.

For each group consider why it might be seen as a good idea and also why it might be seen as a bad idea.

By undertaking this reflection, you may have recognised that you had an initial instinctive reaction as to whether it is a good idea or not. However, by taking the time to consider the problem from a number of different angles you may have realised that the proposal is not as straightforward as it may first appear; there are lots of different areas and potentially differing opinions that need to be explored.

When carrying out your research, you must consider a broad range of views and opinions. You should explore any evidence that supports a proposed approach, but also any evidence that challenges that approach. This means remaining objective and putting your own thoughts and opinions to one side. You should adopt a neutral and objective stance, allowing you to explore a problem rather than simply seeking to confirm any pre-existing beliefs about it. Have a look at the following policing spotlight that explores how researcher bias may impact a study.

POLICING SPOTLIGHT

PC Morris works on a fraud investigation team. Some of his investigations are very complex and require lengthy written reports to be prepared. He feels that it would be more efficient and easier to prepare these detailed reports if he was able to work from home as there would be less distraction than in the office. Therefore, he is doing some research with the aim of identifying the advantages of working from home as a fraud investigator. He has searched for books and journal articles that discuss the benefits that home working can offer. He also knows that several of his colleagues feel the same, so he has selected them to be interviewed as part of his research. During interviews, a couple of his colleagues tell him that they favour working from home, but they can see some disadvantages in it. When PC Morris writes up his research, he does not mention the disadvantages and focuses only on the benefits that home working could provide.

Now have a look at the following critical thinking activity and consider how to approach this research in a more balanced manner.

CRITICAL THINKING ACTIVITY 2.3

LEVEL 6

a) Identify at least three areas where the researcher's bias may be impacting on this study.

b) Identify three things you would do differently and explain why.

Sample answers to these questions are provided at the end of the book.

When you are selecting and reading literature, you need to ensure you are keeping a balance rather than just using or interpreting literature that supports your pre-existing belief.

In designing your own research approach, you also need to think carefully about how you will select participants and obtain your data to try to ensure that it is balanced. In an investigation you would not be expected to just take statements from witnesses that confirm what you think has happened; you would also take statements from witnesses that give a broader view on what happened. Within research, this means you should not just select participants that you know will simply support your beliefs, but you should adopt an unbiased approach to participant selection. This is known as adopting a *sampling strategy* and Chapter 5 explores this in more depth.

Once you have obtained your data and are analysing it, you need to check that you are being fair and open minded in your interpretation of what the data is showing. When the police present a case to the Crown Prosecution Service, they should reveal information that points towards the guilt of a suspect as well as any information that may contradict it. Within evidence-based research this means you need to avoid being selective in what you report. Ask yourself whether you are reporting both supportive and contradictory evidence and ensure you are being balanced.

RESEARCHING WITHIN YOUR ORGANISATION

It is important for the researcher to remain objective and research without bias. However, it is also recognised that researchers will often come with pre-existing knowledge and experiences and therefore will often have their own thoughts and biases. This is particularly true of academic research conducted by practitioners within their own field. This is known as being an *insider researcher* (Brown, 1996). Evidence-based policing research is often conducted by insider researchers because practitioners are uniquely placed to be able to identify problems and then explore and research them.

However, as an insider researcher there is the risk of a preconceived bias. Therefore, you should develop your ability to be able to recognise your own biases and how they may impact on you at every stage in the research process. One of the ways to do this is to engage in *reflective practice*. You should keep a reflective diary throughout your research. In this you should consider not only what you are doing, but why you are doing it. Examine how your own experiences and your own values, beliefs and opinions may be impacting the research you are undertaking. This will support your critical thinking skills and develop you as a reflective practitioner.

SYSTEMATIC EXAMINATION OF EVIDENCE

Investigations rely on the structured gathering of information. Being systematic allows a logical path to be followed. A structure allows you to set your parameters and build your investigation in a planned and ordered manner. You should be organised and plan out your actions.

Within your research this is an essential skill. Planning which sources of material you want to explore, where to find them, how to find them and then how to systematically examine and record them will make your journey as a researcher much smoother. You also need to set parameters to keep you focused on the issue at hand. It is all too easy to drift away from the point but being systematic can support your focus.

IDENTIFYING THE PROBLEM

The first thing to do with any investigative process is to identify what the problem is. Often this involves speaking to a victim or witness to ascertain what has happened. Once the nature of the problem has been identified it is necessary to set some questions to help you examine the problem and then undertake some actions to try to resolve it.

Imagine a situation where local residents have complained about youths gathering in a shopping centre late at night and causing noise and disturbance. You identify the problem as anti-social behaviour in a neighbourhood. You need to ask a number of questions to help you explore that problem. Questions you may consider are:

- who are the youths?

- what are they doing?

- why are they gathering there?

Asking these questions helps you to understand the problem better and allows you to fully consider the appropriate options available to you as an intervention.

This is the same process you will follow in research. First you need to identify what your *research problem* is and then develop your *research questions*. It is important that when you develop your research questions that they are focused, otherwise you will not be able to properly address them. Chapter 5 explores how to develop your research problem and research questions in more depth.

GATHERING EVIDENCE

Once you have determined your research problem and research questions then you need to start looking for sources of information to help you understand the problem better. Within police investigations this is known as setting your lines of enquiry. You identify the different areas where you may be able to gather evidence and then plan how you are going to obtain it. There are two stages to this process, which this chapter will now explore in more depth:

1. what is already known;

2. what else you want to know.

WHAT IS ALREADY KNOWN

Imagine the following situation. A police officer is investigating a report that a 14 year-old child who is in foster care failed to return home. Therefore, the problem that the police officer is investigating is that a young person is missing. The questions that the officer may have include:

* where is the missing person?

* who is the missing person with?

* what risks are there to the missing person?

These questions help to drive the direction of the investigation. The officer initially wants to find out what information is *already known* and available to help him to understand the situation better. In this case, he checks the police databases for any previous reports about the missing person. He speaks to social services to obtain background information. He also checks the guidance documents on investigating children missing from home to help guide his actions.

When the officer is doing this, he is going to a number of different sources of existing information to review what is already known. This allows him to have a clear understanding of the problem he is investigating. It also helps to identify actions the officer could undertake to help him answer his questions and also the best practices to follow.

Within academic study, this search for information that is already known about your research problem is achieved by conducting a *literature review*. Within an investigation you could see how the officer searched for information from a range of sources. Within research you will search for your literature from a range of sources too. Chapter 3 explores the different sources that you may want to explore to find literature that will help you to establish what is already known about your research problem and how it has been approached previously.

Your search for information needs careful planning and preparation. In a missing person investigation, police may want to search a particular area. If the police did not plan these searches and instead aimlessly walked around the area, important evidence may simply not be found. It would also risk duplication of effort if there was no record of how the search had been approached. Instead, the search is carefully planned, a start point is identified, and a methodical approach is taken to ensure a thorough search to maximise efficiency and effectiveness. Within academic research the process is the same. You need to identify the potential sources of information and then develop a search strategy to help you find the literature within your research area. This is explored in more depth in Chapter 3.

WHAT ELSE YOU WANT TO KNOW

Once you have identified what is already known about the problem then you will be in a position to identify any gaps and what else you want to know. You can gather this evidence through conducting your own research.

Going back to the earlier missing person enquiry, imagine that the officer has reviewed the previous reports and has now established that the missing person is usually found with friends. Therefore, he decides that he will now visit the missing person's friends to see if they have any further information. In this way the officer is gathering evidence first-hand rather than relying on previously existing sources of information. Ways that the police gather evidence first-hand include taking witness statements, conducting suspect interviews or conducting forensic examinations.

Within evidence-based research this is called *primary research*. Primary research is the first-hand gathering of evidence. In this phase you are seeking to gather new evidence to help you address your research questions.

Broadly speaking, there are two approaches that you may take to conduct primary research, which are known as *quantitative* or *qualitative*. A quantitative approach tends to be more numerical or statistical, whereas qualitative research focuses on a more subjective analysis of people's experiences.

Within police investigations quantitative data is most similar to the way that forensic evidence is reported. As an example, think about reports you have seen where DNA has been used in a court case. You may have noticed that often a statistical likelihood is given. It may be that the scientists report that there is a one in a million chance of it being someone else's DNA. Similarly, when someone is convicted of drink driving you will see that the police provide a figure for the amount of alcohol in the breath. In this way, this type of evidence is quantified and can be objectively measured.

On the other hand, qualitative data is about gathering people's experiences. Within police investigations this is most similar to witness accounts. It is about a person's observations, what they experienced, what they saw, what they thought and what they felt. This type of evidence relies on someone's perception of what happened. Therefore, this type of evidence is subjective.

Chapter 5 explores the concepts of quantitative and qualitative data in research in more depth. It also introduces you to the research methods that you can use to gather these types of data.

EVIDENTIAL EVALUATION

Evidence is the body of information that tends to support a notion or belief. Within policing there are rules about what can be introduced and used as evidence within a court of law. The rules for academic research are not as strict; you can draw on a wide range of material to discuss but some types of evidence may still be considered better than others.

WEIGHTING OF EVIDENCE

In an investigation, information can come from variety of different sources. However, you may give more weighting and ascribe more value to some types of evidence. To start thinking about this, complete the following reflective practice activity.

REFLECTIVE PRACTICE 2.2

LEVEL 6

Imagine a case where you have arrested a man on suspicion of burglary. You have a statement from his girlfriend saying that he was at home with her on the night of the burglary. However, you also have the suspect's fingerprint on a windowsill outside the broken kitchen window.

- Evaluate which of these two sources you think is more valuable to your investigation.

- Explain why you have valued the information in the way you have.

In the above example you may have been tempted to say the fingerprint was more reliable because it is more objective. However, the fingerprint does not prove the burglary, it merely shows that at some stage the man has been outside the house. You may place less value on the girlfriend's statement because of her relationship to the suspect and that she may have a motive for providing him with a false alibi. However, her relationship does not necessarily mean that she is lying.

You can see from this example that you would need to do some more enquiries to help you understand what the two types of evidence actually mean for your investigation. If you also obtained CCTV footage showing the suspect in the street of the burglary at about the time of the offence, then you could use this as supportive evidence in combination with the fingerprint. In this way you can see how you can overlay different pieces of evidence to help you develop a more comprehensive picture.

By conducting that exercise, you are already starting to weigh up the relative strengths and limitations of each piece of evidence. This is exactly what you need to do in academic research. Analyse the evidence to understand it, consider its strengths and limitations and understand how it fits together with the other sources; understand what it is actually telling you and importantly what you cannot tell from it. You will do this during the literature review and also once you have gathered your primary data and are analysing it.

Throughout your research you need to decide how much weighting you are giving to each piece of evidence.

- How reliable is it?

- Is there corroboration?

- Is it supported?

- Is it objective or subjective?

- Can you triangulate your findings from different sources?

It is only by examining your evidence carefully and with a critical mind that you will be able to truly understand what the evidence is telling you.

EVIDENCE-BASED POLICING

The polygraph is used as a tool across different parts of the world to help to detect deceit by measuring physiological changes in the body's behaviours. It is not admissible as evidence in England and Wales though because it is not considered to be 100 per cent reliable and a range of effectiveness has been reported (National Research Council, 2003).

However, it is used as a tool to support the management of some sex offenders. As part of the ongoing drive to support evidence-based policing, an evaluation was undertaken of the police use of polygraph testing on convicted or suspected sex offenders (Wood et al, 2020). The evaluation found that there was an increase in the amount of useful new information that was revealed by suspects and offenders.

This study really highlights the importance of understanding what the literature is actually saying. On the face of it, you may simply consider that the polygraph is an effective tool. However, you should be asking why it is effective in these cases. It is interesting to note that most of the disclosures in this study were made in the pre-polygraph interview phase. In these cases, it was not the actual test revealing deceptive information. Instead, the researchers proposed that the thought of the polygraph may motivate interviewees to disclose information. Therefore, the perception the offender has of what the polygraph can do may be relevant. This shows the value of understanding the data in front of you and questioning what it is really telling you.

PRESENTING EVIDENCE

Finally, you need to think about how you will present your research. In a police investigation, if a report was prepared that was full of the opinions of the investigator without supporting evidence then it is unlikely to proceed any further. Everything you report needs to be evidentially based; you should have a way of showing why you are making the points that you do. Within an investigation, you will use your statements, CCTV and forensic results to evidence your report. Within academic research, you will need to reference the literature you have read to support the points you are making. You will also use your primary research findings, but you need to accurately report those findings even if they contradict your initial beliefs about the research area.

Within an investigation, you should expect the police officer to present a balanced and professional report at the conclusion of the investigation. The report will be reviewed by others and it is important that the information is conveyed in a clear, concise and precise manner. Similarly, within an academic report you need to recognise that it is a professional piece of work. Therefore, your language needs to be formal and professional. This does not mean using long, overly complex or unusual words; rather, it is about conveying your information clearly so it can be understood by your audience but avoiding casual or informal language. For further details on writing up your research see Chapter 6.

TRANSFERRABLE SKILLS

This section outlines the skills required in both investigations and the research process. Consider the following policing spotlight.

POLICING SPOTLIGHT

As a police officer I was doing investigations every day. When I started university study I felt really disorientated and was unsure what was expected of me. However, I quickly learned that my work-based investigative skills really helped me. I realised that research is about identifying a problem and exploring it. In my work I am used to weighing up the strength of different types of evidence and information and this is exactly what I needed to do when evaluating academic evidence too. I also found that by doing research it really developed a lot of my skills and by the end I felt that it had actually also made me a better investigator.

Now complete the reflective practice activity to explore your own feelings as you begin your journey as a researcher.

REFLECTIVE PRACTICE 2.3

LEVEL 6

Reflect on your own research journey and evaluate your thoughts on the following questions.

- How confident do you feel as a researcher and why do you feel that way?

- How do you think your investigative skills could help you as a researcher?

As you have read through this chapter, you should have noted that there are a number of skills that are transferrable between investigative practice and the research process. The final part of this chapter summarises those skills, emphasising the similarities between the skills needed to conduct effective investigations and those needed to conduct effective evidence-based research (see Table 2.2).

Table 2.2 Transferrable skills

Skill	Description
Critical thinking	The ability to be able to objectively assess information, think broadly and maintain an open and questioning mindset.
Problem solving	In order to effectively solve problems, it is necessary first to define what the problem is and then explore the potential solutions. Using an evidence-based approach to problem solving enables a more robust and effective approach.
Planning	Take the time to plan your approach, what you want to achieve, your potential sources of information and how you could gather information. Also predict potential problems or barriers and plan for contingencies.

$\longrightarrow$

Table 2.2 *(continued)*

Skill	Description
Organisation	Being able to organise material so that you can systematically explore it is vital. You need to consider how you will store information and how you will keep track of what you have done and what you have left to do. This helps you to avoid repetition, and also makes sure that you have a logical and ordered approach to dealing with the material and making sense of it.
Time management	Within any investigative process you are likely to have time limits to manage. Within policing this may be the custody timeline, court deadlines or just managing your caseload within the confines of your tour of duty. Within academic research, you are most likely to be governed by your assignment deadline. You need to be able to plan your time to ensure you use it effectively. It is advisable to develop a proposed timetable of events to help give you a focus and a realistic expectation of what you need to do.
Analysis	Being able to analyse the material and data you have gathered to make sense of it and understand it is key. Being able to weigh up the reliability and relevance of the material you have gathered, objectively assess it and use the best available evidence to support your arguments is core to effective investigation and research.
Writing	Whether you are preparing a report for a criminal investigation, for a court trial or for academic research, you need to be able to write in a logical and accessible format. The presentation, style and accuracy of your writing will all help you to get your message across. Writing in an objective manner where you present the material logically and clearly supporting it with evidence will make your reports balanced but impactive and informative.
Influence and negotiation	In order to influence and negotiate outcomes with people, you need clear and rational lines of argument. Understanding practice through research allows you to develop a depth of knowledge to support your arguments. It can be a powerful tool when consideration is being given to how to approach a particular problem. Presenting evidence-based arguments allows a more informed and robust approach to be adopted.

CONCLUSION

This chapter has introduced you to thinking about research as an investigative practice. It has drawn on the similarities between work-based investigations and evidence-based research, highlighting the importance of critical thinking, systematic examination and evidential evaluation. Finally, it has explored how the skills needed for effective investigations mirror the skills needed for effective research and how you can use them within evidence-based policing.

SUMMARY OF KEY CONCEPTS

This chapter has discussed some of the following key concepts.

🔧 **Critical thinking:** maintain a curious mindset and always question the evidence that you find.

🔧 **Bias:** evidence-based research is about what you can evidence; it is not based on your opinion or personal experience.

🔧 **Systematic examination:** research should be planned and conducted in a structured and methodical manner.

🔧 **Evidential evaluation:** there are lots of different types of evidence and you should evaluate each source to assess how much weighting you will give it.

🔧 **Transferrable skills:** the skills you develop as a researcher will support your work as an investigator and vice versa.

CHECK YOUR KNOWLEDGE

1. Identify two similarities between an investigation and evidence-based research.

2. List three transferrable skills that are required as an investigator and also as a researcher.

3. Explain what critical thinking means as a researcher.

4. Explain how bias can impact on a research project.

5. Explain why it is important to adopt a systematic approach to gathering evidence.

FURTHER READING

BOOKS AND BOOK CHAPTERS

Copley, S (2011) *Reflective Practice for Policing Students.* Exeter: Learning Matters Ltd.
A good book that explores the value of reflective thinking for the policing student.

Costley, C and Fulton, J (2019) *Methodologies for Practice Research: Approaches for Professional Doctorates*. London: Sage.
A useful book that explores your position as an insider researcher and how to recognise your own biases.

WEBSITES

College of Policing (2021) Investigation Process. [online] Available at: www.app.college. police.uk/app-content/investigations/investigation-process (accessed 15 January 2022). The College of Policing provide further information about how to systematically structure an investigation and the skills required.

CHAPTER 3
IDENTIFYING EXISTING EVIDENCE

LEARNING OBJECTIVES

AFTER READING THIS CHAPTER YOU WILL BE ABLE TO:

- distinguish between the different types and sources of evidence available in the existing literature;

- locate evidence held and produced by different agencies, societies, organisations and policing commentators which produce research and information concerning evidence-based policing;

- apply search strategies to identify and locate material available online and offline;

- utilise your university library and the National Police Library;

- navigate between online and offline sources of information and track down articles which are unavailable online.

INTRODUCTION

There is an enormous amount of existing research material available for you to find concerning issues across the breadth of law enforcement. The trick is knowing where to locate that research, which means understanding the different places where you can find it. This chapter will help you to do that by categorising the wealth of sources available to you and suggesting strategies you can use to search for them.

The aim of this chapter is to focus upon resources linked to evidence-based policing (EBP). It will enable you to distinguish between source types and to understand the breadth of existing evidence. This includes online and offline sources, work-based and academic literature, publicly available official sources, legislation and case law (decisions usually stemming from Court of Appeal cases). Focus will also be upon identifying societies, organisations and independent commentators relevant for EBP, not forgetting the various business and corporate agencies which either fund research or conduct it themselves. We have put this information into nine Resource Pillars, which will assist you to identify where you need to search for your research project information.

SEARCHING FOR EXISTING MATERIAL FOR YOUR PROJECT

The way you search for material is very important. Most people search for information using search engines such as Google, Yahoo, Bing, Yandex and others. Each search engine is not the same and you may get different results from each one. If you conduct a search using EBP as the search term, the results will reflect only those sites which have information on what EBP means or represents. Research into EBP can be on a wide variety of policing issues and it is likely that the majority of it will not be termed EBP.

Try and develop the habit of using more than one search engine. They use different algorithms which present slightly different results. Each algorithm searches in a different way and by using keywords in a different order (Thelwall, 2007; Lewandowski, 2012). This explains why search results will vary.

It is natural to begin by searching for the central topic such as fraud, crime prevention, human trafficking, roads policing and so on. You should receive 'hits' on most things you search for. That does not mean you have found everything. The way in which you search the internet also affects the amount of relevant 'hits' you will obtain.

Deploy your search strategy using keywords: this is usually a better way to search and is dependent on the words you choose to use. Each time you add a keyword, the parameters of the search are tightened up. You begin to hone your search to discover the subject material you require. Remember that a search engine is designed to put the most relevant results first. That does not necessarily mean the initial results are the most relevant. Search engines such as Google, Yahoo and Bing usually provide a user guide on how to refine your search techniques. Some private sites offer the same advice (Emerald Works, 2021; Search Engine Journal, 2021). It is a good idea to familiarise yourself with such user guides so that you can search for information more effectively.

CRITICAL THINKING ACTIVITY 3.1

LEVEL 4

Think about how you search the internet. Imagine you have been tasked with an EBP project about crime prevention in the UK.

a) Write down the number of results if you search using the words *crime prevention research*.

b) If you search again but using the words *crime prevention research UK*, what happens? Does the number of results reduce to a manageable number?

c) Search again using *crime prevention research UK Midlands* and see if there is a further reduction.

d) Finally, conduct a search using *"crime prevention research UK"*. What is the result? Notice the search terms are now enclosed in double quote marks. This means that you are searching for the exact phrase only.

You should find that the results have pared down to just one. By conducting this simple activity, you should now understand a little more about how search engines work. Remember that enclosing your search terms in double quote marks eliminates a more general search.

Sample answers to these questions are provided at the end of the book.

RESOURCE PILLARS: CATEGORISING EXISTING RESEARCH

In recent years, a lot of EBP research has been conducted and it is not always clear where information and resources are retained. It is very important to use recognised sources for information relevant to the concept of EBP, which is now a remit recognised to not only include policing issues but also policing processes, policy, practice, management issues and the organisational aspects of policing (Brown et al, 2018). This includes academic articles and grey literature (information not produced by commercial publishers, for example, government and research reports, working papers, conference proceedings, business and industry research projects). To identify the different types of reliable EBP research that is currently available, we have created nine Resource Pillars describing organisations and the information they hold and which might assist you in your project. They represent a starting point for your search for information and are not intended to list every avenue available to you.

You may find research to assist you in more than one Resource Pillar.

1. **G**overnment agencies.

2. **A**cademic literature.

3. **L**aw enforcement.

4. **A**vailable toolkits.

5. **C**ollaborations.

6. **T**hink tanks.

7. **I**nternational organisations.

8. **C**harities, societies, voluntary organisations and the business sector.

9. **C**ase law.

You can remember the Resource Pillars by applying the mnemonic GALACTICC.

Each Resource Pillar provides information about the types of organisations included within it and the information they are likely to hold. Please remember that the lists and descriptions within each of the Resource Pillars represent a guide to searching for EBP research. They are not exhaustive lists of what is available, and there may also be more than one Resource Pillar which is relevant to your research.

Access points to the Resource Pillars are generally three-fold:

1. online;

2. university library;

3. National Police Library.

WHAT DO THE RESOURCE PILLARS CONTAIN?

Each of the nine Resource Pillars contains information relevant to EBP in two aspects.

1. Research information generated within the UK and relevant to its domestic policing agenda, or research information connected to international law enforcement issues and policy.

2. Research information generated outside of the UK, but which is in some way relevant to its domestic policing agenda or to international law enforcement issues and policy.

'RAIDING' REFERENCE LISTS

No matter where you are searching or what you are searching for, remember to check the reference list at the end of any documents or books you discover. Reference lists are invaluable sources for identifying previous research on the subject you are interested in and will lead to further research and information which you can use. This process of finding related research is sometimes called *reference chaining* and is a common practice. Very often you will begin your search and only discover one or two documents appear to be available. Check the reference list as a matter of habit and you will be surprised how quickly your search for information progresses. If you discover articles from using this technique which are older or a little more obscure (because of specific content), you may find that they are unavailable online. If that is the case, then use your university library or the National Police Library to track them down for you (see the Library section below).

REFLECTIVE PRACTICE 3.1

LEVEL 4

Choose an aspect of policing and then search on the internet to identify any journal articles on the topic.

- Open the article and scroll to the end. Have a look through the reference list and familiarise yourself with the research literature the author consulted in order to write the article.

- Check out the references used and if you select any of them notice that they will contain their own reference list, and so on.

You will notice that none of the Resource Pillars include newspaper articles, television programmes or social media posts. These are not usually considered to be reliable sources (for EBP or other research areas) and should not be used except in the rarest of cases. Such articles can be written to sensationalise a specific issue; they can be one-sided, misinformed or biased from social, political or economic perspectives. A TV programme or a newspaper article may highlight an issue or give you an idea to research. They may point to other information on a subject but for EBP (or any other academic purpose) they should be avoided where possible. There are usually academic articles, books or properly conducted research material available which you can use in your EBP project.

RESOURCE PILLAR 1: GOVERNMENT AGENCIES

GOV.UK

The singular online source as a starting point to search for EBP information in the UK is the Gov.uk website (www.gov.uk/government/organisations). It contains a comprehensive list of 23 ministerial departments and 20 non-ministerial departments. A ministerial department is led by a minister who is a Member of Parliament and usually chosen by the Prime Minister to do so. The policies which govern much of the law enforcement priorities in the UK originate from these departments.

Non-ministerial departments are usually led by a senior civil servant. Such departments usually carry out a regulatory or inspection function (Gov.uk, 2021).

We have included some examples of the two types of departments in Table 3.1 for you. It is important to remember that in addition to these types of departments, Gov.uk also lists a further 300 agencies and public bodies which may be of use depending upon what information you are searching for. You will be able to identify and access these from the site.

Table 3.1 Examples of ministerial and non-ministerial government departments

Ministerial departments	Non-ministerial departments
Cabinet Office	The Charity Commission
Department for Business and Energy	Crown Prosecution Service
Department for Digital, Culture, Media and Sport	HM Revenue and Customs
Home Office	National Crime Agency
Department for Environment, Food and Rural Affairs	Serious Fraud Office
Department for Work and Pensions	UK Statistics Authority
HM Treasury	Competition and Markets Authority
Ministry of Defence	Supreme Court of the United Kingdom

HOME OFFICE

Although included in the list of ministerial government departments, the Home Office is worth a mention in its own right because it leads policy, decision-making and research concerning crime, policing and terrorism within the UK. The site contains a lot of reliable EBP law enforcement research which you can access for research projects.

CRITICAL THINKING ACTIVITY 3.2

LEVEL 5

Formulate a search strategy for EBP research into deaths in police custody.

a) Identify where you would search for information and then consider where the most accurate information is likely to be stored.

b) Once you have made a decision as to where to search, try entering the search parameters into a search engine and see where the trail leads.

Sample answers to these questions are provided at the end of the book.

COLLEGE OF POLICING

Besides being an operationally independent '*arm's length body of the Home Office*' (College of Policing, 2021h, p 1) the College of Policing shares knowledge and good policing practice. The College of Policing website is an excellent place to find links to other organisations, EBP research and current policing policy and practice. You will see various links to the College of Policing used in the nine Resource Pillars where appropriate. The links we describe for you demonstrate some of the information available for your research project.

NATIONAL CRIME AGENCY (NCA)

As explained in Table 3.1, the NCA is not a police force. It is a non-ministerial government department and is primarily responsible for protecting the UK public by targeting serious and organised crime. Its website contains a variety of links to EBP source information and research. Searching the site is different to some government sites.

CRITICAL THINKING ACTIVITY 3.3

LEVEL 5

You are asked to locate statistics or information about the UK national strategic threat assessment regarding serious and organised crime.

In any research task, think critically about what you are being asked to do.

a) This task is about the 'national' strategic threat assessment so think critically where you are most likely to find the information.

b) Try searching for the information when you have made your decision as to where to look and compare your strategy to ours at the end of this book.

Sample answers to these questions are provided at the end of the book.

INTERNATIONAL RESEARCH ASPECT

Don't forget that research on a lot of the issues you might be expected to research to enhance UK policing also takes place abroad. There are many law enforcement agencies throughout the world that have been, and continue to be, involved in research. If we consider a topic such as the use of police body-worn video cameras, a search of the internet using simple keywords *"police body cameras"* quickly reveals EBP research in countries besides the UK. The United States, Australia, the European Union and New Zealand are just some of the places where EBP research into the issue of body cameras has taken place. Now you know it is out there, you shouldn't miss it when your research begins.

The Washington State Institute for Public Policy is a good example of a non-UK government policy-making organisation (United States). It is responsible for many research projects in the United States, which may be of value to research initiatives in the UK. It is easily found by searching its name or going to the website: www.wsipp.wa.gov/CurrentProjects.

RESOURCE PILLAR 2: ACADEMIC LITERATURE

There are many sources available where you can locate academic literature and research concerning policing issues. In addition to books, journal articles tend to be the preferred method by way of which academic researchers publish their material. This is because most journals are peer reviewed.

Peer review is a recognised process whereby an article is submitted to a journal for publication and is independently reviewed by other individuals in the same research area. The significance and validity of the information contained in the article are assessed and, based upon the assessment, a decision is made whether or not to publish it. If the article is considered to be of poor quality or contains invalid information, it will not be published. Such a system ensures articles are original and of good quality, which is why they are relied upon by researchers and academics.

Journals are available on an array of subject material and can be used to underpin the research you are conducting or to challenge results. If you are not a member of a university or other research organisation, you can subscribe to journals so that you receive copies electronically or by traditional post. The easiest way to locate and obtain this type of material is to search online if you are just trying to locate one article. You may be able to obtain a full copy from a website or you can usually order any article (free) from your university library, through an inter-library loan system. Each journal tends to have its own website where you can search in specific or general terms either by author, by subject or by title.

RESOURCE PILLAR 3: LAW ENFORCEMENT

Although it has a growing catalogue of research articles in many areas of policing, not all research conducted within law enforcement or by police forces is held by the College of Policing. In the last decade, practitioner–research partnerships have been developed in many countries so, once again, be prepared to search a little wider for information. Sometimes you can find unpublished articles online which can lead you to extensive reference lists of other material, even if you are not using the original article or report, for instance, Alpert et al (2013). The article submitted to the US Department of Justice may not have been officially published but it serves as an example of a very extensive literature review of academic and practitioner research potential. The central point is that although you may initially be drawn to primary websites such as the College of Policing and others mentioned within this chapter, you should never treat them as the sole source of information.

Don't forget to consider what other organisations connected to policing have to offer. For example, if you were considering a project about deaths occurring after police contact, research and statistics would be available from the Independent Office for Police Conduct (IOPC), although this is not necessarily the first place you might think of to look.

RESOURCE PILLAR 4: AVAILABLE TOOLKITS

There are many online resources which you can use to locate EBP research. Most have been specifically designed to help collate and identify relevant data and information pertinent to advancing policing practice. These toolkits categorise subject material so that you can search for specific subject areas within the broader title of EBP. Toolkits can be offered within any of the Resource Pillars and usually provide structure, advice and methods to be utilised when conducting EBP research or evaluating it.

Examples of toolkits include the following.

- **Policing Evaluation Toolkit** (College of Policing, 2021a) – resources to evaluate EBP and the extent to which a strategy has been successful.

- **Crime Reduction Toolkit** (College of Policing, 2021i) – summary of best available research regarding 'what works' to reduce crime. This is probably one of the first sources to check for information as the College of Policing is the central repository for information about UK policing.

- **Online Resources** (College of Policing, 2021j) – links to other research tools on the reduction of crime. Includes links to the Society for Evidence-Based Policing, the Global Policing Database and other useful approved EBP websites.

- **Knowledge Hub** (Policing's National Collaboration Hub, 2021) – research collaboration between the public and private sector. The site provides access to

College of Policing published research on a variety of policing issues. EBP research projects are ongoing in many areas of policing.

- **Burglary Prevention Toolkit** (Neighbourhood Watch, 2021) – police-approved site offering online materials. Additional information can be found in Resource Pillar 8.

- **SHERLOC** (Sharing Electronic Resources and Laws on Crime) – this is a knowledge management portal from the United Nations Office on Drugs and Crime (UNODOC). It provides information about international policy, legislation, case law (Appeal Court decisions), treaties and transnational organised criminality (UNODOC, 2021).

- **Crime Prevention and Criminal Justice Tools Catalogue** – provides a consolidated list of handbooks on policing and criminal justice issues. Each handbook provides information relative to researching particular areas of law enforcement and the criminal justice systems worldwide (see Resource Pillar 7 for more on the UN). This is a good example of a toolkit developed at international level which may offer relevance and insight for specific research projects undertaken from a UK perspective.

RESOURCE PILLAR 5: COLLABORATIONS

POLICE AND ACADEMIC PARTNERSHIPS

There are numerous such collaborations in the UK (College of Policing, 2021e). Their common core priorities are to: focus upon real-world policing problems; innovate research-led solutions to professional policing practice; and translate research results into effective and sustainable policing practice. The following policing spotlight explains why collaboration is useful.

POLICING SPOTLIGHT

The East Midlands Police Academic Collaboration (EMPAC) is a partnership between five constabularies, relevant police and crime commissioners and seven universities. The idea of such collaborations is to integrate professional and academic expertise to address a broad array of policing issues. It also ensures that research projects about any aspect of policing in the five counties are not duplicated. The collaboration acts as a centralised checking point, which benefits researchers and policing objectives alike. Suppose you want to conduct research concerning how drone technology can be used in policing. You would submit your research proposal to EMPAC for two reasons: first, to check whether other similar research is being or has been conducted and second, to register your own project and add it to their database of research.

It is important that you do not just rely on the College of Policing site for information. Once you know a collaboration exists, you can search the relevant university site for additional information, in particular for the journal articles produced as a result of EBP research. If you cannot access the full article (sometimes only the abstract and reference list are available), you will be able to request a copy via your own university library.

Other examples of information sources include the following.

- **Campbell Collaboration** (www.campbellcollaboration.org) – an international social science research network for many aspects of society including crime and justice (Campbell Collaboration, 2021). It also has its own publication capacity in the form of a peer-reviewed online journal, the *Campbell Systematic Reviews*.

- **Police Knowledge Fund** (https://whatworks.college.police.uk/Partnerships/Knowledge-Fund/Pages/Police-Knowledge-Fund.aspx) – a two-year project between the College of Policing, Home Office and Higher Education Funding Council for England. A £10 million fund supported 14 police–academic research collaborations involving 39 police forces and 30 academic institutions across the UK.

- **Society of Evidence-Based Policing** (www.sebp.police.uk) – simply put, this is a society of policing and research professionals whose objective is to improve policing using EBP. Membership is free and an application can be made using the website at: www.sebp.police.uk/membership.

RESOURCE PILLAR 6: THINK TANKS – RESEARCH-LED INSTITUTIONS

Remember that crime is a global problem and there are many organisations which conduct research into areas of criminality worldwide. Not all EBP research is based in the UK. Nor is all research commissioned by universities, government departments or law enforcement agencies. The examples provided here should demonstrate that some organisations exist as non-profit entities which approach law enforcement issues from a moral perspective and desire change to allow law enforcement to work more efficiently and effectively. Below are a few examples of organisations which conduct research and feed into government policy here in the UK and internationally.

- **Basel Institute on Governance** (https://baselgovernance.org)

  Focus: a not-for-profit institute which conducts research regarding aspects of law enforcement, corruption, public and private governance and compliance.

Also comprises an International Centre for Asset Recovery, which is part funded by the UK Foreign, Commonwealth and Development Office.

- **Royal United Services Institute (RUSI)** (https://rusi.org)

    Focus: financial crime and security studies (fraud and terrorism, bribery and corruption), defence industry and international security studies, organised crime and policing, terrorism and conflict, cyber security (RUSI, 2021).

- **Transparency International UK (TI-UK)** (www.transparency.org.uk)

    Focus: this is a branch of a global organisation, primarily an independent anti-corruption organisation, which feeds information into different areas of policing. Research conducted by TI-UK is used to inform UK government policy in many areas of policing, particularly serious and organised crime, serious fraud, bribery and corruption. Its research is also used to understand issues such as global financial flows from drug trafficking and money laundering and to lobby for additional law enforcement powers (TI UK, 2016).

- **The Rand Corporation** (www.rand.org)

    Focus: non-profit organisation conducting research programmes in 50 countries. Conducts research on many subjects. In the context of EBP, includes policing issues of cybercrime, national security, terrorism and others.

This Resource Pillar continues to highlight that many organisations constantly conduct research, which then goes on to inform government policies concerning law enforcement. There are many such organisations worldwide which you can use to inform research projects.

The important point to note is that if you had conducted a search using 'evidence-based policing', you may have missed the Basel Institute and the other organisations mentioned in this Resource Pillar altogether.

RESOURCE PILLAR 7: INTERNATIONAL ORGANISATIONS

International organisations have conducted a lot of research in recent years, and it is important to understand that much of it relates to laws and policies currently active in the UK.

This section deals with four significant international organisations which continue to influence policing in the UK; they are responsible for driving the concept of EBP worldwide to enhance the effectiveness of law enforcement practice.

UNITED NATIONS (UN)

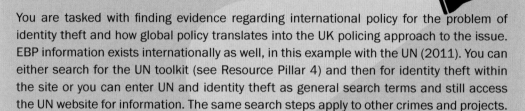

POLICING SPOTLIGHT

You are tasked with finding evidence regarding international policy for the problem of identity theft and how global policy translates into the UK policing approach to the issue. EBP information exists internationally as well, in this example with the UN (2011). You can either search for the UN toolkit (see Resource Pillar 4) and then for identity theft within the site or you can enter UN and identity theft as general search terms and still access the UN website for information. The same search steps apply to other crimes and projects.

FINANCIAL ACTION TASK FORCE (FATF)

The Financial Action Task Force (www.fatf-gafi.org) is an inter-governmental body which effectively acts as the global watchdog for international money laundering and terrorism. Recently it has turned its attention to the threat of digital assets and has various research publications concerning economic criminality, illegal financial flows, anti-money laundering regulations and associated matters. Although not seemingly directly connected with routine EBP in the UK, the FATF is largely responsible for recommendations which have led to changes in UK law regarding money laundering, fraud and wider economic criminality and the methods by which assets can be dealt with around the world. The FATF is a good example of how globally agreed recommendations and research projects on such issues can feed into routine UK policing.

INTERPOL (INTERNATIONAL CRIMINAL POLICE ORGANISATION)

INTERPOL (www.interpol.int/en) is an international and inter-governmental organisation which has 194 current member states. It has its own INTERPOL Innovation Centre based in Singapore. Its objective is to bring together academics and law enforcement officers to develop cutting edge responses and approaches to combat international criminality (INTERPOL, 2021).

EUROPOL

EUROPOL (www.europol.europa.eu) is responsible mainly for supporting European Union member states in fighting terrorism, cybercrime and serious and organised crime. EUROPOL also works with non-member EU countries as well as many international organisations. Conferences on these issues are routinely organised and research papers of speakers who participate are published on the EUROPOL website (EUROPOL, 2021).

RESOURCE PILLAR 8: CHARITIES, SOCIETIES, VOLUNTARY ORGANISATIONS AND THE BUSINESS SECTOR

Various groups and organisations exist within the global and national business communities. They have a vast amount of data regarding all types of criminality and crime prevention measures (including about the internet and the challenges it presents for business and law enforcement). Extensive research is commissioned by the business and charity sector, not only for business reasons. Various studies have taken place into many aspects of criminality and the potential crime prevention measures to combat them (Crawford and Evans, 2017; Brennan, 2019). There are also several business collaborations which have been created to engage with law enforcement to combat the more serious and organised criminality in the UK and internationally. Some of these are mentioned below.

It is worth knowing these groups exist and although not strictly think tanks they are hubs where reliable facts, figures, information and up-to-date news on trends in crime can be accessed. As officially recognised organisations which work with law enforcement when the need or opportunity arises, they are useful to approach for data and assistance with your policing research project.

When referring to the business or private sector, it is advisable to use information from government-recognised sources such as those listed below (there are of course others). Avoid referring to blogs and posts from companies which are not usually considered reliable source material.

Many businesses and financial institutions want to assist law enforcement to uncover serious criminality because it is in their interests for trade and commerce to do so. They frequently conduct their own [policing] research projects and, where they can do so, they are quite willing to work with law enforcement as it is in their own interest to do so. If you are conducting a research project, these types of businesses represent a bank of current data and information to help you as well as networking opportunities to discover other avenues and repositories of information. Here are some examples of relevant organisations.

- **Cifas** (www.cifas.org.uk) – this is an example of a non-profit-making fraud prevention membership organisation. It has over 400 organisation members including the Home Office (Resource Pillar 1), the Legal Services Commission, the Financial Conduct Authority and the UK Border Agency (Cifas, 2021). Cifas demonstrates how the various groups and organisations mentioned in this chapter are integrated with each other on some level.

- **International Association of Financial Crimes Investigators (IAFCI)** (www.iafci.org) – a group which was formed in the United States initially within the private sector, and now has other 'chapters' around the world, including Europe. Originally established as a network for the exchange of law enforcement and private sector intelligence, it is an organisation which has access to the latest national and international statistics, trends in criminality and its own EBP, largely concerning fraud, money laundering and financial crime.

Other UK groups which have been created for business and law enforcement intelligence interchange and co-operation include the Anti-Counterfeiting Group, the Police Foundation, and the Joint Money Laundering Intelligence Task Force. All of these groups conduct research projects into aspects of law enforcement and policing.

- **UK Research and Innovation (UKRI) (previously the Economic and Social Research Council [ESRC])** – this type of organisation conducts research nationally and internationally. It is often not strictly from a law enforcement perspective so why do we mention it? Take a look at their website (www.ukri.org) and you will see it uses social science research projects to feed into government policy making, local authority strategies about economic growth, unemployment, law, politics and international relations. There is also some helpful information which explains the difference between qualitative and quantitative research (see Chapter 5). At any one time, the UKRI supports over 4000 research projects in academic and independent research organisations (Resource Pillars 5 and 6) (UKRI, 2021). Although not specifically dealing with policing in its own right, this type of research will underpin most local policing issues and shapes public policies, law and wider societal issues. These are fundamental issues with which policing is connected and most evidence-based research is related to.

- **Neighbourhood Watch (2021**) – a charitable organisation supporting individuals and communities to create safer communities. Responsible for EBP research projects concerning crime prevention in the UK, locally, regionally and nationally.

RESOURCE PILLAR 9: CASE LAW

The UK criminal and civil courts and tribunals system is not straightforward.

Criminal and civil cases may both start at the Magistrates' Court and can proceed to the Crown Court, the High Court, the Court of Appeal and if necessary to the UK Supreme Court. Tribunals can proceed from a First-tier Tribunal through its own system but still end up at the Court of Appeal or the UK Supreme Court (Courts and Tribunals Judiciary, 2021).

If as a result of any court proceedings a point of law is disputed, the matter may be referred to the Court of Appeal for a decision to be made. Thus, case law (sometimes referred to as 'stated cases') is made by judges who make decisions on issues raised by the lower courts (tribunals, magistrates and crown courts) by interpreting the laws laid down by Parliament. In other words, a panel of Appeal Court judges create a legal precedent with their decision, which then has to be adhered to in similar cases on similar points of law.

Once a case law precedent is set, it cannot be easily altered. As you search through case law decisions you will find there may be many decisions involving a particular area of criminality or civil law. Consider fraud as an example. The term is a broad one, so it is not surprising that as thousands of fraud cases pass through the courts, many different issues and points of law are required to be decided upon by the Appeal Court.

Remember that case law exists in other countries as well. Using the United States as an example, you could locate case law relevant to US legislation via the online Library of Congress for example (Library of Congress, 2021). Other countries have similar mechanisms available for you to use.

WHY IS CASE LAW RELEVANT TO RESEARCH?

POLICING SPOTLIGHT

Consider the broad issue of money laundering within the UK. If you conducted research into this subject, it would be useful to know the legal context of money laundering in the UK before you begin to formulate a research plan (as explained in Chapter 5). Money laundering is defined within the Proceeds of Crime Act (2002) (POCA), which would be your starting point. The question is whether, since 2002, there have been any changes to the legislative definition or the intent behind it. This is where case law kicks in. One case, *R v Anoir* [2008] EWCA Crim 1865 substantially affected the way in which money laundering prosecutions could be made. Where POCA seemed to deal with money laundering related to a specific offence (linking money to the actual crime, such as a specific human trafficking offence for example), the Appeal Court determined that it was legal to prosecute for money laundering connected to a form of criminality (not the specific offence where the money may have been made as this might not be known). Various conditions would apply to any such future prosecution of stand-alone money laundering as determined and stated by the Appeal Court. The effect of the judgment essentially made it easier to charge and prosecute money laundering offences where the crime could not be identified but the type of criminality could be (fraud, drug trafficking, human trafficking etc).

SOURCING CASE LAW

With over 50 case law databases available online for UK cases, searching for a specific case can be a bewildering exercise if you do not know where to start searching when search engines such as Google and Yahoo do not prove fruitful. There are many websites now available to direct your attention to case law databases, such as www.accesstolaw.com. It is generally accepted that the most comprehensive archive of UK case law online is stored by the British and Irish Legal Information Institute (BAILII), which also stores case decisions made in Ireland, the Commonwealth and Europe (BAILII, 2021).

CASE LAW REFERENCE SYSTEM

If you know the reference given to the stated case you require, it makes searching easier.

POLICING SPOTLIGHT

Using *R v Anoir* [2008] EWCA Crim 1865 as a guide, case reference numbers (called citations) generally consist of the case name, which includes both sides of the case. In our example, *R v Anoir* means Regina versus Anoir (the defendant on Appeal). The name is then followed by the year in which the appeal case was decided upon by the Court. The year is usually enclosed in square brackets. EWCA Crim simply means the England and Wales Court of Appeal, Criminal Division. 1865 is the judgment number.

There are many online sites which contain information about case law referencing. A helpful website that is simple to read is available from the University of Oxford: www.law.ox.ac.uk/legal-research-and-mooting-skills-programme/law-reports.

THE UNIVERSITY LIBRARY

Find out about what your university library offers online and offline. As a member of a university, you will be given online access to library resources, tools and workshops. Your faculty will usually have a single point of contact at the library to direct any queries to or to ask for help in researching articles, papers and books. If you find an article online but cannot access it, your university library usually has the capacity to obtain it for you, electronically or otherwise.

LIBRARY ONLINE ACCESS

There will be remote and direct access to the library, usually through your student portal. This normally allows you to remotely order books and articles for collection or in the form of electronic books and journal articles which you can download and access for a limited period of time via your own computer. If you discover an article online but can only access the abstract and reference list, this is a great way to access the full material and at no cost to yourself.

Remember that not everything is available online. Take an online tour if one is available but there is no substitute for a visit to see what is available and meet the librarian who can explain and show you what is available. We recommend a visit to the library because although 24/7 online access offers you flexibility, it does not substitute for leafing through a wide spectrum of books and articles relevant to your research topic.

SUMMARY OF KEY CONCEPTS

This chapter discussed some of the following key concepts.

- **Wider perspectives for EBP:** research is not only the concern of governments and law enforcement. In addition to collaborations between law enforcement and academia, many companies and organisations invest in research relating to policing issues and make the results of such research available to public scrutiny.

- **Utilising all available resources:** do not just search for EBP information, and think beyond what the College of Policing might have to offer.

- **Breadth of research:** availability of research is widely spread between different organisations, which all have different reasons and perspectives regarding why research is conducted and invested in.

- **International relevance:** research conducted in other countries may be relevant to UK policing and government strategies and is easily located.

- **Search strategies:** the way in which you search online for information may affect the results of your search.

- **Resource Pillars:** by quantifying the different areas where research can be located, your search will adopt a more systematic approach (GALACTICC).

- **Traditional pathways:** the university library is always available to track down articles which are otherwise difficult to obtain.

CHECK YOUR KNOWLEDGE

1. How many Resource Pillars are there and what is their function?

2. Why are keywords important when you search for information online?

3. Why is the university library important if you are searching for information primarily online? Think of a subject and explore the online library systems to gain experience in navigating them successfully to locate what you need.

4. What is the reason for raiding reference lists in existing research articles?

5. Why is it important to use more than one search engine when searching online?

FURTHER READING

BOOKS AND BOOK CHAPTERS

Gravelle, J and Rogers, C (2014) *Researching the Police in the 21st Century*. London: Palgrave Macmillan.

Knutsson, J and Tompson, L (eds) (2017) *Advances in Evidence-Based Policing*. New York and London: Routledge.
Two good books that explore the concept of EBP.

JOURNAL ARTICLES

Brown, J, Belur, J, Tompson, L, McDowell, A, Hunter, G and May, T (2018) Extending the Remit of Evidence-based Policing. *International Journal of Police Science and Management*, 20: 38–51.
This article considers what may constitute 'best-evidence' and proposes other considerations and areas for EBP to cover. The effect of a wider evidence-based policing avenue offers increased potential in developing the PEQF framework and isolating research gaps.

WEBSITES

College of Policing (2021) Support. [online] Available at: https://whatworks.college.police.
uk/Support/Pages/Support.aspx (accessed 15 January 2022).
The College of Policing support website for advice on EBP.

CHAPTER 4
ANALYSING EXISTING EVIDENCE

LEARNING OBJECTIVES

AFTER READING THIS CHAPTER YOU WILL BE ABLE TO:

⚙ effectively manage and review the existing literature discovered for your research project;

⚙ apply reading and note-taking strategies to systematically review and evaluate the literature you have found;

⚙ apply critical thinking skills when reading and analysing information;

⚙ understand the source or origin of material, its validity and reliability;

⚙ identify how evidence fits together to confirm or deny conclusions from material being used and how recommendations can be made from it.

INTRODUCTION

Chapter 3 helped you to identify existing sources of information (the Resource Pillars). In essence, this chapter offers practical advice on critiquing available literature. It develops your skills to manage the information you find on a particular project and how to systematically review, record and critically analyse that information: in effect, a literature review of the existing evidence available on any given subject. This includes some note-taking strategies you can use to identify the important points in the information you find before considering what critical thinking means and how to develop it as a skill, as in the policing spotlight example.

Just because a statement is made in a book or article, it does not mean it is factual, correct or true. Similarly, in a policing environment, a witness making a statement about an event does not mean it is correct, accurate or true. Critical thinking is an important thought process for you to employ in both fields in order to ask questions about the information provided to you, what type of information you are looking at and its veracity. Towards the end of the chapter, our attention focuses on what the term 'best evidence' means in a policing context, and why verifying the source(s) of your information (referencing) is important.

CRITICAL THINKING ACTIVITY 4.1

LEVEL 5

The Battle of Hastings was fought in 1066 AD. The Normans won. The Saxons lost. The Normans were a superior fighting force.

These are four simple statements, the first three of which are historical facts. All four statements tell us very little about that event in history and whether the Normans really were a superior fighting force.

Apply a critical thinking process to the three facts and the statement about the fighting ability of the Normans.

a) Write down at least three questions you would ask that would begin to unpick the information.

b) Considering these questions, examine the accuracy of the statement that the Normans were a superior force, possibly challenging that conclusion. You can apply the same method of thinking to the literature you identify for your EBP project.

Sample answers to these questions are provided at the end of the book.

MANAGING INFORMATION

In the previous chapter you became aware of the various sources of information about all types of policing and law enforcement that exists for you to discover when undertaking an EBP project. Before guiding you through managing the information you find, consider the next policing spotlight feature, which explains how to approach the selection of articles to read.

POLICING SPOTLIGHT

CONSIDERING THE PROJECT

Imagine you are tasked with a research project with the objective of ascertaining whether new drone technology available to police forces replaces the need for Force helicopters. Think about the aspects of drone technology that might be relevant. Using the Resource Pillars in Chapter 3 as a guide for information, some of the issues you may search for may include articles about:

- the technology itself;

- any research already conducted regarding the public reaction to using drones;

- any links to the media coverage of drone usage (positive or negative press);

- the cost of drones versus helicopters;

- the effectiveness of drone technology versus helicopters;

- the access to drones within police forces (will it be only specialists that can use them?).

Approaching your research project in this way (the list is not exhaustive) will guide your reading and your search for information. You will then be able to more easily identify any gaps in the literature about the use of drone technology in policing. This will help you to focus your efforts on obtaining primary research data to address those gaps and perhaps influence policing using an evidence-based approach (see Chapter 5).

As you perhaps expected, some sources (whether they are national or international) are directly connected with or generated by law enforcement, some are academic, some are outside of the public sector and some are a result of government policy or directives. In view of the many sources of information available to you, whatever research project you undertake, managing the results of your search may prove disparate or confusing without a structure to keep your reading and note-taking relevant to the objectives you initially set. There are certain key elements to ensure you keep track of what you have read and the usefulness a source may have for your project. These elements apply whether you use pen and paper records or spreadsheets and technology.

First and foremost, you should avoid information overload and deal with a few sources at a time. A good tactic is to have the objectives of your research displayed where you can remind yourself of them at all times. It is easy to distract yourself by pursuing information which may be interesting but is not useful to your project, thereby diverting you away from your goal(s) and wasting time.

Here are some tips for keeping on top of the sources of information you find.

- Develop a spreadsheet or table that records the book, author and publishing details plus a free-text space in which you can note the pertinent points for your project within each article.

- Always record your sources in an alphabetical order according to the referencing system you have chosen or been assigned to use. This will prove invaluable in larger research projects and the collateral benefit is that you are already compiling a reference list to use in the finished project.

- Write a brief summation of what you have read either during or immediately after you have finished reading. If you have many sources of information, it is surprising how you can read something which later proves important, but you cannot remember which source you were using. Very frustrating!

A systematic review of the literature pertinent to your EBP research project is always essential. The end objective of your review will be to confirm, deny or modify (add to) the existing literature in order to influence positive changes to evidence-based practice. This is the goal of your project: to inform policing practice and enhance it where possible. It makes sense that your review will be focused upon areas within the subject field which are the most useful to your project (Gronmo, 2020).

POLICING SPOTLIGHT

Imagine you are researching an aspect of intelligence or intelligence application and there is no shortage of existing information on the subject in available articles, books and other published materials as well as online information. As you collect your material, you are able to systematically manage your various sources by including their details and relevance in a table (see Table 4.1).

Table 4.1 How to record what you have read and its relevance to your project

Reference	Information type	Synopsis and relevance
Ratcliffe, J H (2009) *Strategic Thinking in Criminal Intelligence.* 2nd ed. Sydney: The Federation Press.	Book	Edited series of intelligence commentators. Good insights into UK developments in intelligence (Chapter 3) and the theory and practice of intelligence collection (Chapter 6). May be something to use in Chapter 8 – exploratory intelligence tools.
Ratcliffe, J (2010) Intelligence-led Policing and the Problems of Turning Rhetoric into Practice. *Policing and Society*, 12(1): 53–66. [online] Available at: www.tandfonline.com/doi/abs/10.1080/10439460290006673?src=recsys (accessed 15 January 2022).	Article – available on internet	Intelligence-led policing (Australian based). Not much here for this project except the influence that political and media rhetoric plays within the intelligence field.
Richards, J (2010) *The Art and Science of Intelligence Analysis.* Oxford: Oxford University Press.	Book	Chapter 1 deals with intelligence definitions. Great chapter on tactical use of intelligence – page 156. Consideration of the intelligence environment – context for political, cultural and ethical influences on intelligence.
Casciani, D (2020) New Rules for MI5 and Police to Authorise Crimes. *BBC News*. [online] Available at: www.bbc.co.uk/news/uk-54274605 (accessed 15 January 2022).	Internet BBC News piece	New law enabling police to commit crime while intelligence gathering.

Not only does a table or similar method of recording material make it easier for you to deal with multiple sources, it provides a library of information which you can archive and use again. A table can be as extensive as you think is necessary or practical, with more columns than the example here. We have kept our notes section brief just to demonstrate to you how to complete a table. You can put as much as you think is relevant in the notes section and it is a good way of condensing articles into the bullet points you need to remember. If the article you have read is online, you may decide to hyperlink it from the table you create. The possibilities are endless and you can suit your own needs in a methodical and comprehensive manner. It also makes it easier to construct a bibliography or reference list for your project as you can simply copy and paste the ones you have used within your research.

READING STRATEGIES

How we read documents has changed a lot in recent years. Printed texts are now equalled, if not surpassed, by the volume of devices upon which we are now able to access material through the digital environment, for example, iPads, smartphones, Kindles. Each brings its own challenges, but a general rule of thumb is to recognise the purpose of the text, whether it is on- or offline. Your aim is to identify the most relevant and up-to-date texts pertinent to your project and it is widely acknowledged that you should give some thought to your reading surroundings. Always be aware that articles you find on the internet may not have been properly reviewed and may be unnamed so always verify the source before using (Afflerbach and Cho, 2010).

You will probably absorb more information in a quiet environment than you would in a busy café where distractions are likely. It is important to think about what you are reading and where you are reading.

The next policing spotlight provides some general advice on how to develop a reading strategy.

POLICING SPOTLIGHT

Imagine you are tasked with enhancing or improving an existing policing framework such as the National Intelligence Model (NIM), which is the broad structure used by all UK law enforcement to sanitise, process and act upon intelligence possibilities. The first thing to do will be to determine the extent of the existing literature about intelligence and the NIM. Refer to the Resource Pillars in Chapter 3 for where you might start to find information and then you may want to consider the following tips which will make your search for information a comprehensive one.

- Journal articles usually have their title and an abstract available, which provide a synopsis of what the text is about. If you find 50 articles on a subject, this is an excellent way to sift through what is or is not relevant to you.

- Books usually contain a preface or a back cover summation which explain what the book is about.

- Introductions and conclusions usually provide important information to introduce or summarise what is being written about. These offer a way to quickly get a 'feel' for a document and if they seem relevant, you can read the text in a more 'in-depth' fashion.

- Check out the contents page of books and journals to quickly find texts you might be interested in. This will give you an overall feel as to whether something has relevance to your research objectives.

- Research articles usually have a recommendations section, which provides insight into where any gaps in the literature might be. This may influence how you approach your primary research (see Chapter 5).

If you locate a large amount of information on a subject, think of a few key words you can look for in title headings, journal titles, government policy and strategy documents and even media headlines. This will make scanning the material to find the relevant ones much easier.

Every stage of this advice allows you to establish an overview of a text and its potential relevance or usefulness to you before you commit to properly reading it and using precious time unnecessarily.

NOTE-TAKING STRATEGIES

When you are reviewing the documents and texts you have discovered for your EBP project, one of the most important skills to develop is note-taking in an effective, structured and clear way. Various note-taking methods are available and, as there is not enough room here to consider all the alternatives, more information is provided in the further reading section at the end of the chapter. This section provides an insight into some of the available strategies you can apply to make note-taking much more effective and extract the central points from the text to write an assignment or project.

Note-taking can now be accomplished in two environments: in a traditional manner where you read and make handwritten notes, diagrams or mind maps, or online where the dominant method is probably using a highlighting function, which is available in most software. If you later use a quote from a highlighted online text then it is a simple process to copy and paste, making sure you always reference properly and accurately.

Both methods are equally viable, and it is a personal choice depending upon which you are most comfortable with. The strategies to make your note-taking more effective in either environment are largely the same.

Whether you write in the margins of a copied document or book you have purchased, annotate, underline or highlight the text itself, or whether you use any form of handwritten notes, it is deciding what you intend to highlight or note which will make the task much easier. You should also avoid copying out long tracts of texts. The skill is recognising the key points or quotations within the text which are best suited to the research you are undertaking. These are the points you need to highlight, and which can be expanded upon in your completed review of the literature. It is these points which you can summarise in your records table, as demonstrated in Table 4.1.

POLICING SPOTLIGHT

Imagine you are conducting research concerning how the public in your Force area regard the use of drone technology for policing purposes and have identified 50 different sources which appear relevant to your project. Consider the following points of advice and think about how they might apply to how you would make notes on such a large number of texts.

- Avoid distractions when you are concentrating on your project.

- Don't just copy out the bulk of the text again. Use your own words so the meaning is clear to you. Be selective about what you are recording and summarising as not everything will be relevant to you.

- Are you attempting to identify facts and figures, research themes, definitions, policy decisions, theories, arguments and debates (or any other specific point)? Think about why you are making the notes in the first place and therefore how much detail you need in them.

- Identify key words or phrases which are most relevant to your objective. Most reference systems such as Harvard recommend using short quotes in your work so avoid writing out quotations which are longer than 40 or 50 words (as a rule of thumb).

- If you identify different themes in your reading, try using different-coloured pens so that you can quickly identify relevant points when you are writing your project.

- Indicate in your notes whether authors or research data are in agreement. If texts or researchers disagree, can you see where and why there are differences while you are making your notes? This ties in with the critical analysis sections of this chapte. Critical analysis is about what it all means and why. Critical analysis will be easier because you have already applied critical thinking while note-taking.

- When you have completed your notes on a text, read them through to be certain they make sense. There is nothing worse than coming back to your notes to find they no longer make sense to you. Be orderly at all times.

Something which is often overlooked is what you do with your notes when you have made them. If you are working directly in a digital environment (on a computer or other device), please ensure you know exactly where you have deposited your notes. It is important to devise a clear and easy-to-follow archiving system. If you are working offline, on photocopies or annotating in books or articles you have bought, ensure your notes are clearly written and then stored where you can easily find them.

Think about all of the strategies you have just learned and undertake the next critical thinking activity.

CRITICAL THINKING ACTIVITY 4.2

LEVEL 5

Imagine you are researching drone technology. Read the following paragraph taken from an article abstract (Custers, 2016) and consider what you would highlight.

Aside from the drone itself (ie, the 'platform') various types of payloads can be distinguished, including freight (eg, mail parcels, medicines, fire extinguishing material, flyers, etc) and different types of sensors (eg, cameras, sniffers, meteorological sensors, etc). Applications of different payloads will be described. In order to perform a flight, drones have a need for (a certain amount of) wireless communication with a pilot on the ground. In addition, in most cases there is a need for communication with a payload, like a camera or a sensor. To allow this

→

> *communication to take place frequency spectrum is required. The requirements for frequency spectrum depend on the type of drone, the flight characteristics, and the payload. Since frequency spectrum does not end at national borders, international coordination on the use of frequency spectrum is required.*

Sample answers to these questions are provided at the end of the book.

CRITICAL THINKING

The term 'critical thinking' causes many students some degree of anxiety but in reality it is simply a term which means you should look at what is being presented before you question the context, meaning and source of the information. This section builds upon what you learned in Chapter 2 about critical analysis/thinking. First, there is no single definition of the term 'critical thinking'. For the purpose of EBP, and put simply, it means not accepting information, ideas, observations and arguments at their face value. In other words, a critical thinker is inquisitive and at the same time tries to be aware of any personal bias which could affect the research project being undertaken. Information should not be passively received (as in the example at the start of this chapter). A good researcher questions the data and is '*persistent in seeking results which are as precise as the subject and the circumstances of inquiry permit*' (Facione, 1990, p 2). Think about the statements made concerning the Battle of Hastings at the start of this chapter. A critical thinker moves beyond what is being described and accepts nothing at face value.

THE LITERATURE REVIEW

For any project you are undertaking, it makes sense to begin by explaining the evidence base in relation to the subject under discussion. A good start is to appraise the reader about the current literature (the evidence base) which is available. Is there a lot of literature on the subject; is there an abundance of studies? If so, are the studies (research) in agreement and if not, you must comment on what the differences appear to be (this is critical analysis). Is there a paucity of research (not much seemingly available) on the subject matter and, if so, why might that be?

Don't just describe. Critical analysis without doing your own primary research (explained in Chapter 5) is about what you can determine from the existing and available literature.

One way to look at this is that you as the author are the tour guide for the reader. Imagine you are on a tourist bus and are pointing out to the reader the relevant places to visit (the important points within the literature). At each stage of the journey, you will explain to the reader the information you have discovered in the literature, what it means, its reliability or contradictions and whether you feel there might be other places to visit which are not currently on the route (gaps in the literature). You can use a fact or figures but then explore what the fact or figures might mean (positive or negative). While you are doing this, are areas revealed where you can suggest in your conclusion that there appear to be gaps in the available literature? In completing the tour of the literature for the reader, you can then recommend what needs to be done to fill those gaps (any ideas for further research).

THE 5WH METHOD

This section enhances information about the 5WH method, which was initially provided in Chapter 2. Within a law enforcement environment, probing witness accounts of an event utilises what is commonly referred to as the 5WH method. Particularly in a policing context, questions such as who, what, why, when, where and how can be key levers to use to unpick information and delve beneath what is being described on the surface. It is an easy method to remember as you develop your critical thinking skills.

Applying a who, what, why, where, when and how approach to literature effectively presents you with a recognised and solid framework to apply critical thinking to any subject. On any research project you undertake, it is a process you can apply to confirm, deny or modify (identify gaps and make recommendations) the information you have gathered. As a police officer or other law enforcement investigator (just as in academia), critical thinking is a fundamental process for sifting through information, intelligence and evidence.

As a critical thinker, you can alter your approach depending on what information is being examined and can deploy various evaluation questions and adapt them to the research project as required.

CRITICAL THINKING ACTIVITY 4.3

LEVEL 5

Imagine you are conducting a literature review about police attendance at routine patrol crime scenes. You discover the following passage, which at first sight appears to be presented as indisputable.

⟶

Police have been 'rumbled' by the public for their failure to investigate everyday crimes such as car theft and burglary, a watchdog has said. Forces' inability to pursue some of the most common offences has eroded the relationship between police and the people they serve, according to a senior figure in the inspectorate.

Before you commit to using the information in your EBP project as a reference, what are your considerations? Apply critical thinking to the statement and write down some of the questions you might ask as to its validity and accuracy. (So as we don't give anything away in this exercise, the paragraph citation is at the end of the book to acknowledge the source it was taken from rather than here where it normally would be.)

Sample answers to these questions are provided at the end of the book.

Applying the sorts of questions you are thinking about allows you to start to critically analyse the literature you have discovered or the data you have collected. The skill is not to destructively challenge what is in front of you. The whole point of critical thinking is to move towards a deeper understanding of the subject being investigated (Richards, 2010).

Critical thinking does not just apply to established literature. It is a thought process which will apply to any primary research you might conduct as part of your project. Where you use primary research (data you have collected in addition to the literature review), there are many factors to account for which are outside the scope of this chapter (see Chapter 5).

You will apply critical analysis to the things you describe in your work. In other words, you will comment upon what you are describing with facts and figures – what do the facts or figures indicate? What do they mean?

Similar to conducting a literature review, don't just describe.

Critical analysis (without doing your own primary research) is about what you can find and determine from the literature, so don't forget that you as the author are the tour guide for the reader, as explained earlier in this chapter. You can use a fact or figures but then explore what the fact or figures might mean (positive or negative). While you are doing this, are areas revealed where in your conclusion you can suggest apparent gaps in the research available and recommend what needs to be done to fill those gaps (any ideas for further research)? See the following evidence-based policing example to see how research can consider a problem, identify a 'gap' in practice and recommend a solution to reduce crime.

EVICENCE-BASED POLICING

Consider the problem of pedal cycles being stolen in a particular area. How would an evidence-based research approach be useful in developing a crime prevention strategy to mitigate the problem? In 2010/11 almost 500,000 pedal cycles were identified as being stolen by the British Crime Survey. The problem was considered by the Jill Dando Institute, which undertakes crime and criminology research, and the University of London (UCL). The research identified a potential flaw in the 'n'-shaped bike stands being used in the community and recommended installing what has become known as the CaMden stand, an 'm'-shaped frame which allows both wheels of a pedal cycle to be secured rather than just one. As a result of the research conducted, a 5.4 per cent reduction in cycle theft was recorded the following year (UCL, 2014).

UNDERSTANDING SOURCE MATERIAL

The accepted sources for any research project are usually peer-reviewed journal articles. 'Peer review' simply means that the article you have found has been reviewed by respected commentators and academics in that particular field of study. The system adds rigour so that anyone reading the article can be confident it is accurate and has been researched according to stringent academic standards. The same can be said for books published by established academic publishing companies.

INTERNET INFORMATION

Before we consider internet sources and how to treat them, first try your hand at the next critical thinking activity to begin to understand how to check internet material.

CRITICAL THINKING ACTIVITY 4.4

LEVEL 6

Imagine you are about to begin online research for your project. Spend a few minutes trying to think of the things you might be able to check on screen which you can use to evaluate and authenticate the sources you are looking at.

Sample answers to these questions are provided at the end of the book.

The digital environment (internet) is an amazing place and provides fantastic access to all kinds of research and articles which can be used for your research project. The problem is that it also contains a myriad of misinformation which, if not properly checked and provenanced, can be repeated by unsuspecting researchers as though what they are reading has been properly researched and published. The accuracy of the information you are reading is very important and this is where the critical thinking skills you have learned earlier in this chapter can be applied.

It is important to try and determine whether the information is factual in its account. Is it simply a propaganda exercise, and if so why? What is its objective? Can you identify if the text displays bias or whether it is propaganda? Internet articles usually contain numerous links to other sites and information. When you follow the links, do they take you to sites used for their own agenda or to sites where information can be uploaded by any individual such as Wikipedia? These sites are to be generally avoided.

REFLECTIVE PRACTICE 4.1

LEVEL 4

When trying to ascertain if a site is genuine and credible before you use its content, you are basically checking that the host website is the product of a reputable organisation (or individual).

Choose any university or business website and evaluate the content. Apply your mind to consider whether the content is objective or the site is biased towards that particular institution. What is the author trying to accomplish with the information being presented?

When conducting research online, try to compare and contrast these points to ascertain the objectivity, relevancy and purpose of the information being presented.

Sample answers to these questions are provided at the end of the book.

BEST EVIDENCE AND PIECING INFORMATION TOGETHER

Everything you have learned so far in this chapter is designed for you to be able to find the material (information and evidence), sift through it in an objective and controlled manner, verify the source and accuracy and find any additional material which is referred to in the text (how sources fit together). When you find one source, are there others you can track down; do those sources support each other or not and are they reliable? Repeat the process until you have exhausted the supply of available material. Once you have reviewed and evaluated all of the material you have obtained using the strategies in this chapter, does the information you have found leave questions unanswered that your own research project might be able to answer?

From the start of your information-gathering process, you have effectively been conducting an investigation, whether you realise it or not (see Chapter 2). You have looked for any similarities (or differences) in the available information and have tracked down secondary sources and references used by authors of articles and reports. These are the pieces of your jigsaw and as you employ the strategies in this chapter to your reading and note-taking, you begin to conjoin the material to establish areas of overlap or gaps in the available literature.

In other words, you are establishing the relationships between sources, data, government and local policies and, in the context of EBP, how policing is conducted in any particular theatre of operations. You will then use your conclusions from the review of the existing material to inform your research with a clear idea of the path you need to travel to obtain additional data, why you need to do so and what you need to consider as you begin to do so (see Chapter 5).

POLICING SPOTLIGHT

Imagine that you have returned to work after two weeks on annual leave and your supervisor calls you in to the office to explain there has been a spate of industrial burglaries in the local area. To your supervisor's own knowledge there have been over 20 reports but there may be more. You are allocated the job of collating all of the available information and evidence about the burglaries to identify any intervention action that could be taken to catch those who are responsible. Perhaps the immediate questions you would consider are:

- with so many burglaries to consider, how will you approach the task you have been set?

- what are your considerations?

- how will you manage the information you find?

By applying some of the strategies in this chapter, you would be able to find and record the information in a systematic way. Treat the task much the same as you would treat a literature review and manage the information carefully and logically, as explained above. Compare your approach to the example provided at the end of this book.

CONCLUSION

This chapter has provided you with strategies to cope with unearthing a lot of material for your project undertaking. It has explained how to manage the information you find and how to keep it recorded in concise, relevant terms which you access immediately or at a future time. It has explored critical thinking skills in more depth, building upon what you learned in Chapter 2 and preparing you for what comes next in Chapter 5. It has provided strategies to use for effective note-taking, how to archive your material so you can find it again and, finally, underpinned the imperative that you must check your sources before using them, at all times retaining an objective and enquiring mind. All of the above will facilitate effective research for EBP with the ultimate aim of developing and improving police policy and practice.

SUMMARY OF KEY CONCEPTS

This chapter discussed some of the following key concepts.

⚙ **Managing information:** how to manage large amounts of information by recording it in a systematic and easily accessible way.

⚙ **Application of reading strategies:** how to approach reading individual texts either on- or offline, and the ability to quickly scan certain parts of books and articles to reveal the relevance to your project.

⚙ **Effective note-taking:** developing skills to make effective notes and using time effectively.

⚙ **Critical thinking:** don't just accept what is presented to you. Question everything which you read and apply the basic 5WH method to probe the material and develop good critical thinking skills.

⚙ **Source material:** remembering to check the origin and veracity of source material. Question why the text was written and test its validity by comparison to other research or information.

CHECK YOUR KNOWLEDGE

1. List three things you should remember when you start to take notes from the texts you identify.

2. Identify the quickest way to scan through a book or document if you do not want to read all of the text.

3. Explain the purpose of the tour bus analogy.

4. Explain the words which form the 5WH model and why open questions are beneficial to critical thinking.

5. Explain why you need to check the veracity of source material before you use it.

FURTHER READING

BOOKS AND BOOK CHAPTERS

MacDonald, V (2014) *Notetaking Skills for Everyone: Learn the Strategies of Effective Notetaking in Order to Obtain Maximum Grades Today*. Scotts Valley, CA: Create Space Independent Publishing.

McPherson, F (2011) *Effective Notetaking*. Wellington: Wayz Press.
Two good books that explore the topic of note-taking.

ARTICLES IN JOURNALS

Winchester, C L and Salji, M (2016) Writing a Literature Review. *Journal of Clinical Urology*, 9(5): 308–12.
This article contains strategies which will help you think about how to conduct your literature review.

WEBSITES

University of Reading (2021) Reading and Making Notes. [online] Available at: https://libguides.reading.ac.uk/reading/notemaking (accessed 15 January 2022).
Most universities have information available on their websites to assist students with note-taking, such as the above web page from the University of Reading.

CHAPTER 5
CONDUCTING YOUR OWN RESEARCH

LEARNING OBJECTIVES

AFTER READING THIS CHAPTER YOU WILL BE ABLE TO:

- understand when it is necessary to produce or commission new research;

- formulate effective research questions and produce an appropriate research plan;

- assess different research methodologies and justify the use of a particular method;

- gather and analyse data using appropriate methods, considering ethical requirements;

- write a clear and logical research report with evidence-based recommendations.

INTRODUCTION

The previous two chapters discussed how you can identify and use existing research to help you solve policing problems. This is valuable because it saves you effort if some or all of the work has already been done for you. But what if there is little or no existing evidence or research for you to draw on? Or what if you want to see if existing research findings apply to your local circumstances? The answer is to carry out your own research or ask someone to carry it out for you (called *commissioning* research). You may also want to use research methods to evaluate how effective an activity has been.

Doing your own research might seem quite daunting but in fact it is a bit like following a recipe and draws on skills you likely already have, such as planning a project, asking questions, reflecting on and thinking about your answers, and sharing your findings. The key to doing your own research project is to use these skills in a *systematic* way. The purpose of this chapter is to help you plan and carry out your own research project systematically. Read the evidence-based policing box on the following page to see an example of why this is important.

This chapter looks at how to:

- plan for research;

- ask good questions;

- use different research methods to answer these questions;

- decide on which method of data collection you are going to use;

- analyse your data;

- understand key ethical considerations; and

- write up or share your research in a suitable format.

It serves as an introduction to these ideas and further resources are recommended to develop your understanding.

EVIDENCE-BASED POLICING

Why is using research to inform practice important? Between 1989 and 1992, there was a focus on police interviewing tactics of the past two decades. There were a series of Court of Appeal hearings that saw a number of convictions quashed for terrorism and murder investigations (for further details, see Gudjonsson, 2003). These cases had revolved around confession evidence that had been obtained during police interviews which was subsequently ruled as unsafe.

Therefore, research was commissioned by the Royal Commission on Criminal Justice (see Runciman, 1993) and the Home Office (see Baldwin, 1992) to look at police interviewing standards. Overall, the research identified that the quality of police interviewing was poor; there was little if any preparation, inappropriate questioning and a lack of challenging of suspects' accounts (Baldwin, 1992; McConville and Hodgson, 1993; Williamson, 1993).

As a result of these findings, a working group of police practitioners, lawyers, academics and psychologists collaborated to create the PEACE model of interviewing (Milne and Bull, 1999). A PEACE training package was then developed, piloted and assessed (McGurk et al, 1993) before then being embedded in police learning. The PEACE model was one of the first EBP projects to alter policing behaviours and procedures, and is still the mainstay of victim, witness and suspect interviewing to this day (see College of Policing (2019b) for further details of the PEACE model).

POLICING SPOTLIGHT: SARA

Imagine you are a police officer tasked with reducing burglary and vandalism on a local estate. Your neighbourhood policing team have provided you with some information about where and when these crimes are occurring. How might you use research methods to help you:

1. understand why these crimes are occurring (*analysis*);

2. determine what the best way to reduce these crimes might be (*response*);

3. work out if you have been successful (*assessment*)?

Remember the SARA (scanning, analysis, response and assessment) model from Chapter 1? – this might help structure your answers. Roach et al (2020) addressed a very similar problem to this in Durham so reviewing this paper might give you some ideas.

PLANNING A RESEARCH PROJECT

Good planning can help you in many aspects of your professional and private life, and planning for a research project is no exception. Notice we say *good* planning because there is no such thing as a perfect plan. You cannot possibly know and plan for every eventuality before you begin a project so do not treat your plan as unchangeable. Instead, you should see your plan as something you should revisit regularly and revise as often as is useful to you.

REFLECTIVE PRACTICE 5.1

LEVEL 4

Remember to keep your research as simple as possible. Do not overcomplicate your research project with advanced methods, difficult-to-obtain respondents or complicated sampling strategies, especially if this is your first research project.

- Reflect honestly on your own skill and experience and devise your research accordingly.

- What methods do you feel comfortable with?

STARTING A PLAN

When creating a plan, it can often be helpful to initially write down the date your research findings are needed, for example an assessment deadline or when you are to present your research to colleagues. From this initial deadline you can then work backwards to fill in the rest of your plan.

You will likely need to include the following tasks and activities in your plan:

- developing your research question or questions;

- a literature review;

- gaining ethical approval;

- designing (and perhaps piloting) your fieldwork;

- recruiting appropriate participants (sampling);

- data collection (the fieldwork);

- analysis of your data;

- writing up your findings.

The act of simply listing the activities you need to complete to finish your research project can be very helpful; it serves as a reminder of what is left to do and, just as important for your motivation, what tasks you have already completed. By listing the activities you need to complete you are less likely to forget them.

If you are working on a longer project, such as your dissertation or a long-term project, it may be helpful to plan in terms of weeks and mark on your calendar, diary or planner roughly which tasks you need to have completed by when. You should also include times that you cannot work on your research, such as holidays or other work commitments, which you need to allow for. The key is to be realistic about when you can and cannot work on the research project. Be sure to revisit and update your plan regularly.

ALLOCATING TIME

Different research projects, and different activities within research projects, can take different amounts of time so it is difficult to offer specific recommendations about how long you should allow for each activity. For example, if you are collecting your own data you will need to allow time for this, whereas if you are using secondary data only you may need to include longer for your analysis because it can take longer to clean and prepare the data for your needs. If you need advice, speak to your course tutor or dissertation supervisor who can offer recommendations, or speak to colleagues who have completed similar research before. Your tutors will have a good idea of how long a task will take and will have allowed you plenty of time to satisfactorily complete your assignment.

REFLECTIVE PRACTICE 5.2

LEVEL 4

When drafting your plan, do not underestimate how long it will take to complete a research project, particularly if you have not completed one before. Allow yourself plenty of time; don't leave everything to the last few weeks! Try writing out a realistic timeline for your project and ask a tutor or colleague to review it.

If you are undertaking this type of research regularly, it can be useful to use the Pomodoro technique and track the number of 'pomodoros' each task takes to complete. This will help you estimate the time required for the next project.

STAYING FOCUSED WITH THE POMODORO TECHNIQUE

The Pomodoro technique involves setting a timer for a period of time, usually 20 or 25 minutes. During that time you should concentrate on the task at hand and avoid distractions like email, messages, social media or other work. Once the timer has finished, record a 'pomodoro' against whichever task you were working on and take a short break of three to five minutes and start again. When you have completed four pomodoros in a row, take a longer break of 15–30 minutes.

By recording the number of pomodoros against a task, you can estimate the amount of time it took to complete that task overall, which you can then use when planning for your next research project. For example, if a task took 24 pomodoros, when planning for that task again you will know to allow approximately 10 hours for that task next time (25 minutes × 24 = 600 minutes; 600/60 = 10 hours). You should also allow contingency so you may want to plan 11 or even 12 hours, just in case.

The purpose of the Pomodoro technique is to help you concentrate on the task at hand, avoid distractions and focus for a manageable amount of time. The additional bonus for recording the number of pomodoros is that you can make better estimates about how long a task takes next time you do it.

ASKING GOOD QUESTIONS

The next stage of your research project is developing a small number of connected research questions, usually between three and five. Your project overall will have a problem statement or goal, as outlined in Chapter 1, and your research questions should relate directly to this and allow you to answer it.

REFLECTIVE PRACTICE 5.3

LEVEL 5

Your research questions are different to the questions you ask on your interview schedule, survey or questionnaire. Research questions are the broad questions that guide your project overall, and could be thought of as your aims or objectives, while your interview or survey questions are what you actually ask your respondents.

*   To get a sense of how research questions are stated, review some recent articles in the *Cambridge Journal of Evidence-Based Policing*, which offer a structured abstract with research questions clearly stated.

*   Think about how the research questions you find here could be adapted for your own project. See the Policing Spotlight on burglary below for examples of research questions.

POLICING SPOTLIGHT

BURGLARY

A police officer has been tasked with reducing burglary in a specific area of her local city. She might ask the following research questions to help her address this problem with suitable evidence.

1. Has there been an increase in burglary in the local area?

2. Why has burglary in the local area increased?

3. How can we decrease the number of burglaries taking place?

4. How will we know our actions have been effective?

Note how the four questions are connected and lead from one to the next. In this example, the questions mirror SARA (see Chapter 1), although they do not need to.

*   Question 1 is the *scanning* phase where we identify a problem.

*   Question 2 is the *analysis* stage in which we look at why the crime is taking place so that we can tackle the underlying problem rather than the surface issue.

- Question 3 relates to our *response* and how we should act to reduce the crime or problem identified.

- Question 4 is an *assessment* of how effective our actions have been at reducing the issue.

You may also want to ask if there are already any measures in place; if there are, are these effective and why (or why not)? Adapting or improving an existing measure might be easier and more cost-effective than implementing a new measure, so it can be beneficial to know what is already happening.

To develop good research questions you should start with your original problem statement. You should then narrow your focus and add detail to make your problem 'researchable'. Good research questions should be (adapted from Francis, 2018, p 42):

1. achievable in the time that you have available;

2. answerable with available methods;

3. feasible with the skills you have (or you will need to commission research);

4. relevant and useful to the problem at hand;

5. ethical;

6. clearly defined;

7. of a pertinent nature, such as asking who, what, where, when, which and why.

Good research questions should help you articulate what it is you want to answer and why, and what the purpose of your research is going to be (Green, 2008). Ensure you spend sufficient time developing and refining your research questions; these will guide your subsequent activity on this project, can help ensure you stay focused on the problem, and help prevent you wasting time. As Jupp et al (2000, p 14) state, '*[t]he conclusions of research will be credible and plausible only to the extent to which the questions and problems they address are clearly formulated and expressed and followed through in a consistent manner during the enquiry*'.

CRITICAL THINKING ACTIVITY 5.1

LEVEL 5

Choose a policing problem to focus on.

a) If you are an officer or special constable you could base it on a recent repeated problem you have experienced, or you could use data that is available to you, such as that discussed in Chapter 2.

b) For your chosen problem devise a series of three to five linked research questions that will help you decide what the best response to the problem will be. Remember to make later questions build on and develop earlier questions, and remember it may be helpful to write your research questions in such a way as to mirror SARA.

Sample answers to these questions are provided at the end of the book.

RESEARCH APPROACHES

With your research questions in hand, your next task is to choose and plan the appropriate approach (formally called a *methodology*) to answer these. The methods we choose help us to structure the way we carry out research and the questions we ask in a systematic and repeatable way. The ultimate goal of our methods is to aid our understanding and help us develop theories that explain a particular problem or phenomenon.

Specific theories, such as why young people join criminal gangs, the relationship between unemployment and crime, or the most effective tactics to manage a crowd, are important to help us improve our understanding, summarise our knowledge and communicate our research to others. Different theories will require different approaches (methodologies) to understand and describe them. Broadly speaking, there are two main types of social research approach: *qualitative* and *quantitative*, as well as *mixed-methods research* that combines elements of both in one research project.

Qualitative and quantitative methodologies lend themselves to particular ways of understanding and explaining the world. These are broadly 'subjectivist' and 'objectivist', respectively. A subjectivist world view holds that reality is based on interactions between people and the interpretations they make, and so we should understand these as they are important. This understanding of reality lends itself typically to qualitative research, which has devised methods to explore and describe the meanings in these interactions. A qualitative question might therefore be: 'What is it like to be fearful of crime?'

On the other hand, an objectivist world view is not so concerned with these interpretations, and instead treats reality as something that exists irrespective of how people interact. It is therefore concerned with what can be measured or counted; here quantitative researchers have developed methods to aid with this. A quantitative question might be: 'How many crimes have been committed in the previous 12 months in London?' Table 5.1 summarises some of the key differences between subjectivist and objectivist world views (although it is important to remember that the distinctions are not always so explicit).

Table 5.1 Summary of subjectivism and objectivism

	Subjectivism	Objectivism
Stance	Understand reality by investigating the interactions and interpretations people make	Reality exists irrespective of people's interactions or interpretations
Gain knowledge through...	Exploring what's meaningful to people	Observations or measurement
Lends itself to...	Qualitative	Quantitative
Theory...	Generating (inductive)	Testing (deductive)
Example	What is it like to be fearful of crime?	How many crimes are committed [in an area, in a time period]?

Neither qualitative nor quantitative research is *better* than the other (and we say this as experienced quantitative researchers who have also completed successful qualitative and mixed-methods projects). Instead, they are tools to use in the appropriate circumstances, and one or the other will be best suited to the task at hand. Just as you use a knife for cutting food and a fork for eating, you should choose your research approach based on what you want to achieve.

QUALITATIVE

As the name implies, qualitative research is concerned with the *qualities* of the data. It involves rich description, semi-structured or unstructured questioning, observation, and more open-ended questions that allow your participants to provide a thorough and complete description of their experience or environment. For this reason, qualitative research places a greater emphasis on what is important to the research participants, allowing their priorities to come to the fore. Typically, qualitative research will involve fewer participants (a smaller sample) than quantitative research, but you will ask them for more detailed responses. Questions that qualitative research might be used to tackle include understanding why people offend and reoffend, what it is like to be a victim of a crime, or how police officers respond in a particular situation and why.

Qualitative research most commonly involves research methods such as:

- semi-structured or unstructured interviews;

- focus groups;

- ethnography and observation.

These are explored in more detail later in this chapter.

QUANTITATIVE

In contrast to qualitative research, the focus of quantitative research is on *quantity*. It is concerned with counts or more restricted (closed) questioning. Quantitative methods do not afford respondents the same scope to answer questions on their own terms, but instead afford the researcher a way to collect greater numbers of responses efficiently. Typically, a quantitative project would look to achieve a larger number of responses than a qualitative project. Questions that a quantitative project might ask are how many people reoffend, how many people are a victim of crime, or how many police officers have dealt with a particular problem in a specified time period.

Perhaps the greatest strength of quantitative research is that it allows us to understand the perspective of more people. It does this in part by asking more people in the first place than qualitative research, but it also allows us to infer what the population think (we can generalise if we have sampled correctly). From a sample (our respondents) we can assume that people like our sample would respond in the same or similar ways. For example, if we want to know what police officers think of an initiative, we do not need to ask them all. We can take a representative sample (usually by selecting a sample of officers at random) and asking these individuals only. If we have done this correctly, we can infer what all officers think of the initiative. This is much more efficient and cost-effective than asking everyone.

Common quantitative research methods include:

- surveys;

- questionnaires;

- counts of events (for example, counts of crimes in a particular period).

These are explained in more detail later in this chapter.

MIXED METHODS

Mixed-method research is exactly that: it uses a mixture of qualitative and quantitative research to examine a problem from different perspectives. There are some common mixed-methods approaches which we outline here, but these are not the only approaches that can be taken.

One approach is to begin with qualitative research to explore, describe and understand a problem and what is important to respondents. This information can then be analysed in its own right but can also feed into quantitative research; the qualitative information can help us know what is important to ask and how to ask it. This approach is therefore commonly used when we do not know much about a problem or phenomenon but need to ask quantitative questions. This might be helpful if we want to generate ideas, codes or themes but then test these more formally with quantitative methods.

It is also common to use quantitative research to identify the scale or scope of a problem or phenomenon, then follow up with qualitative research to probe further and understand the meaning or nature of that phenomenon. This allows researchers to gather complementary information and so understand a phenomenon more completely. This is a form of *triangulation*, where a researcher uses two or more approaches to check that the information they are generating complements and corroborates each other, which allows the researcher to be more confident in their findings. Of course, the quantitative element does not have to be completed before the qualitative element of research: it can be the opposite and, in practice, the two may be completed simultaneously and feed in to each other at various points.

CRITICAL THINKING ACTIVITY 5.2

LEVEL 5

Refer back to the research question or questions you devised in the Critical Thinking Activity 5.1 on page 91.

a) Which approach or approaches (quantitative, qualitative or mixed methods) are most appropriate or are likely to be best suited to answer your questions?

b) Why are these the most suitable approaches?

You may find one question calls for one approach but other questions call for a different approach; this is quite common.

Sample answers to these questions are provided at the end of the book.

METHODS OF DATA COLLECTION

Having decided if a qualitative, quantitative or mixed-methods approach is best suited to answer your research questions, the next stage is to decide on the exact research *method* to use. As outlined above, common qualitative research methods include interviews, focus groups or ethnography (observation), while common quantitative research methods include closed questionnaires, surveys or counts. These are not the only approaches, but they are arguably the most commonly used methods and as such are applicable to a broad range of questions and problems. The general steps involved in planning for qualitative and quantitative research are similar regardless of the exact final method used.

INTERVIEWS AND FOCUS GROUPS

Interviews can be structured (follows a prescribed set of questions), semi-structured (has a set of prescribed questions for guidance but can be deviated from) or unstructured (the researcher would typically only have a series of headings). Semi-structured interviews are perhaps the most common method of qualitative data collection because they provide some structure and guidance during the interview process but are flexible enough to allow the researcher or respondent to explore or deviate from the planned questions if other aspects of the topic are important. Interviews allow an element of privacy for the respondent, and therefore respondents might be more comfortable or able to discuss more sensitive or personal topics than in group or public settings.

While interviews concern one respondent at a time and allow great depth of responses, focus groups gather more than one (usually between six and eight) respondents in one activity. Focus groups can be effectively used as a 'group interview', saving time, but are more commonly used to explore how respondents discuss a topic and find meaning as part of a group. '[W]ith a focus group the researcher will be interested in such things as how people respond to each other's views and build up a view out of the interaction that takes place within the group' (Bryman, 2008, p 473).

Carrying out interviews and focus groups typically involves drafting an interview schedule, which is the list of questions or prompts you will ask your participants, and recruiting respondents. This stage is necessary because you would not ask respondents your research questions directly as they will not be expressed in a way that allows this. Instead, you will typically ask a number of questions that help you understand the answer to each research question.

It is good practice to start by drafting questions that help you answer your research question or questions (that you stated in 'Asking good questions', above). A useful technique can be to copy your research questions onto a blank document and underneath each item draft two or three questions that help you answer the overall research question.

You should draft and edit your questions so that there is a logical flow, for example by asking follow-up questions that invite the respondent to answer in more detail or to explain different aspects of an initial question. When drafting questions, ensure you do not compound or stack questions by checking each question asks one thing only. For example, the question 'To what extent do you think knife crime and violence are a significant issue?' is actually asking two questions: one is about knife crime and one is about violence overall. Clearly the two are related but they are distinct activities or offences and respondents may have difficulty answering the question as it is currently worded.

It is also important to ensure your questions are clear and understandable to your respondents by using appropriate language. You may also find it successful to start with easier questions, ask more challenging questions once you have built a bit of rapport with your respondent and eased them into the process, and then conclude with another easier question. For example, if you are interviewing members of the public you might start by asking how long they have lived in the neighbourhood, then ask substantive questions about crime in the area, and conclude by asking if they like living in the area.

Drafting an interview schedule for interviews or focus groups should be an iterative process. You may find it helpful to draft a set of questions, test it on a trusted colleague (who is not involved in the project) or a trusted friend or family member, and make improvements based on their responses. Depending on the complexity of your research you may also wish to obtain a small number of responses and review these for quality. This process is called *piloting*.

With your interview schedule in hand, your next task is to find appropriate people to ask those questions. There are many different ways to sample individuals, called your *sampling strategy*. In qualitative research *purposive sampling* is often recommended so the selected respondents are appropriate to and help you answer your research questions. '*In other words, the researcher samples on the basis of wanting to interview people who are relevant to the research questions*' (Bryman, 2008, p 458). Techniques to attract respondents might include asking known contacts and acquaintances (called *convenience sampling*) or identifying an initial sample and asking these respondents for additional contacts who may be approached for your research (called *snowball sampling*). Convenience sampling is, as its name suggests, convenient, while snowball sampling can be an effective strategy to access hard-to-reach groups. The disadvantage is that these sampling strategies are not representative and do not allow you to make conclusions about a wider population.

ETHNOGRAPHY AND OBSERVATION

Ethnography is a process of the researcher embedding themselves in a site or setting of interest for an extended period of time, often days or weeks. Data collected is primarily through participant observation, but can be complemented through other methods such as interviews. The following policing spotlight illustrates how researchers use interviews and observations to understand the 'choreography' of activities in the setting they are researching, in this case that of probation teams. Ethnography therefore requires '*skills in observing, participating, interviewing, listening, forging relationships, communicating and adopting a role and identity within the research setting*' (Hall, 2018, p 388). The journal *Policing and Society* has two recent special issues dealing specifically with ethnography in policing (Bacon et al, 2020a, 2020b).

The process for ethnography or observation is very similar. For ethnography and observation, planning will involve selecting sites (settings) and contacting individuals and organisations for permissions. If you are planning to carry out interviews as part of your ethnography then you will obviously need to design an interview schedule, as described above. You will need to select appropriate sites to gather data that helps you answer your research question, and you will need to gain relevant permission to access the site. You will also need permission from the individuals you are looking to observe.

POLICING SPOTLIGHT

AN ETHNOGRAPHY OF PROBATION SERVICES

Ethnography has been used successfully and appropriately in criminology for years, but a recent study by a researcher at the University of Sheffield used ethnography to study changes to the probation service (Robinson, 2018). Using observation over 13 days and 21 semi-structured interviews, the researcher was able to explore the 'choreography' of the probation teams and the difficulties and successes of supporting the work of the court. This is a good illustration of how 'behind the scenes' functions in the criminal justice system can be investigated and understood.

1. Do you think other research methods would have been as effective at uncovering the 'hidden' aspects of probation work?

2. Why did the researcher use interviews as well as observation?

SURVEYS AND QUESTIONNAIRES

Surveys and questionnaires are a common method for a quantitative approach and involve asking respondents more closed questions than for a qualitative interview. The responses available to people answering your survey will be more limited and restricted, but it means you can ask more people and efficiently analyse the data. As with interviewing, you will need to identify respondents (your sampling strategy) and devise your questions ready to send out.

Sampling can be representative or non-representative. A representative sample will allow you to make inferences to a wider group of people who have not completed your survey (the population). The simplest representative sample is a simple random sample, where everyone in the population has an equal chance of being selected. For example, if you want to know what all police officers think about a topic (your population is all police officers), you would obtain a list of all officers and randomly select a subset (your sample) to complete your survey. Based on these answers you can infer what all officers think, without having to go to the cost and complexity of asking everyone.

A non-representative sample does not allow us to make this inference, but can nevertheless be useful as it can be simpler and cheaper to administer and can be used even if it is not possible to obtain a representative sample. Of course, we should not claim inferences about a wider population as this sort of sample might not necessarily represent the views of everyone we are interested in. A non-representative sampling strategy might be to post a survey to social media or hand out a survey at the local supermarket: these are not random samples (you do not know who will see the survey on social media; the people in a supermarket at a particular time of day will not be random) but can be very useful in some circumstances.

When devising quantitative questions there are a few common question types that can be used. Our role as researchers is to use an appropriate question type that asks the right question but that keeps the survey overall as short and straightforward as possible. Question types include Likert scales (for example, strongly disagree – disagree – neither agree nor disagree – agree – strongly agree), simple yes/no, a 1–5 or 1–10 scale, or a simple numerical count ('how many times have you been a victim of crime in the last 12 months?'). Therefore, it is important to match the question you wish to ask and the most suitable way to allow respondents to answer. It can be a useful approach to examine previous questionnaires, for example the *Crime Survey for England and Wales* (ONS, 2021), to see how other researchers approach particular questions and base your own questionnaire on these.

CRITICAL THINKING ACTIVITY 5.3

LEVEL 5

Take your research questions and research approach that you developed in critical thinking activities 5.1 and 5.2 and devise a series of questions that you might ask respondents. These will likely be interview or focus group questions if you are using a qualitative approach, or survey questions if using a quantitative approach. You may wish to start by copying your research questions onto a blank document and filling in two to three survey or instrument questions under each.

Sample answers to these questions are provided at the end of the book.

The final step for both qualitative and quantitative research is to have a sense that we are asking the right things and, consequently, obtaining the 'right' answers. Having drafted your interview schedule or survey questions (or both) it is important to check the quality of our questions, which we discuss in the next section.

INDICATORS OF QUALITY

It is important to have a sense of the quality of your research. Specifically, you want to know two things: if you are measuring what you think you are measuring (validity) and that you can repeatedly measure the same thing (reliability). Clearly you need to ensure you are measuring what you set out to measure: it is no good if you believe you are measuring one aspect of crime or victimisation but your respondents are providing answers to a slightly different question, for example because of ambiguous wording in your questions. Similarly, you want to avoid the situation where a respondent answers a question one way, but answers related questions in an entirely different way (called *internal reliability*, although it should be noted that there are other forms of reliability).

For example, imagine we ask the following two questions: 'To what extent do you agree or disagree that punishments for convicted burglars should be harsher?'; and 'To what extent do you agree or disagree that punishments for convicted drug dealers should be harsher?' We might reasonably expect that most respondents will answer both questions similarly, because they either think punishments should be harsher in general, or they do not. This would probably be the case if the answer scale for both questions was the same (strongly disagree – disagree – neither agree nor disagree – agree – strongly agree), but if we reversed one scale we might reasonably expect many of our respondents to miss this and answer the two questions very differently. Our questions would suddenly have poor internal reliability.

As a basic check of the validity and reliability of your measures, you might opt to ask other researchers with familiarity in the field you are researching whether your questions or measures make sense and are appropriate. You may also consider including two or more similar questions to determine if respondents are answering in approximately the same (or at least a consistent) way. For example, you might ask what respondents think about sentencing for two or more different types of crime. Assuming respondents will be generally more or less punitive in their outlook, their responses should be relatively consistent and this will increase your confidence that your measures are reliable. By also asking experienced colleagues, you can also increase your confidence that your measures are valid.

Validity and reliability can be applied to both quantitative and qualitative research, and are therefore worth considering regardless of your chosen research methodology. In addition, or as an alternative, many authors propose a slightly different set of criteria for qualitative research, including *trustworthiness* and *authenticity*. If you are considering qualitative research you may wish to explore these; see further reading.

ANALYSING YOUR DATA

Once you have gathered your data you are going to need to analyse it to identify patterns and consistencies, as well as explainable difference in those patterns. This section introduces you to methods of analysis, but you will need to refer to your course tutors or additional reading on research methods for further information.

If your research has used qualitative methods, you will likely analyse your data for themes, called *thematic analysis*. The general process is to review your detailed notes or transcripts and label sections of text that relate to the concept you are studying. For example, if you have carried out a series of interviews on why certain households were burgled, you may find responses that indicate a lack of concern for physical security, such as respondents indicating they left their windows or doors unlocked. You could code these instances as 'poor security' across the series of interviews you carried out. Once you have coded (labelled) each interview, you can then review these looking for patterns or reasons why respondents answered as they did. In this way, your analysis generates theories to explain why things happen in the way they do; this is sometimes referred to as *grounded theory* in the literature.

Analysis for quantitative methods takes a more numerical and statistical approach. Generally, you will look to identify patterns and similarities, but by comparing *variables*. For example, you might compare ethnicity against the likelihood of being a victim of crime. Such analyses might indicate that respondents who are Black or Black British are more likely to be victims of crime than White British respondents (Gov.uk, 2020). It is common practice to begin by analysing each variable individually using the mean (average), median or mode. These provide a single value that summarises the variable, and are referred to as *descriptive statistics*. You can then compare more than one variable by producing frequency tables or cross-tabulations that show you the relationship between these variables. Finally, you can progress to performing simple statistical tests. We do not have the space to discuss all these here, but have listed some recommended reading at the end of this chapter to help with your analysis.

ETHICS

Before you begin any fieldwork you will most likely need to gain ethical approval from your organisation. If you are completing a dissertation your university will require you to gain ethical approval, and your module tutor or supervisor can help you with this process. Within the police you will also be required to obtain ethical approval before beginning formal research. Ignoring these ethical requirements may lead to harm to your research participants, as well as reputational harm to you and your organisation.

Regardless of the process of gaining ethical approval, you will need to consider the same aspects to ensure your research is completed to a high ethical standard. Gaining approval is important but we have a moral and legal obligation to ensure our research is ethically sound and of a high quality. It is not possible to discuss all ethical requirements and eventualities in this chapter so you should seek specialist training or support from a suitably qualified individual in your organisation to understand what is required of you, but we outline the main issues here.

ANONYMITY

Your respondents should have their identity protected so they cannot be identified from your research. This is important since it protects respondents' safety and privacy, as well as improving the quality of your research by encouraging fuller responses. Researchers typically manage this by using a unique code to identify the individual respondent (usually a unique number) or by using a pseudonym (fake name) if quoting respondents in a final report.

CONFIDENTIALITY

To further protect the identities and privacy of your respondents, you should also ensure their data is treated in confidence. This means, as a minimum, not sharing data with individuals outside the research project team (for example, a supervisor) and storing data securely using appropriate encryption. You should speak to your IT department to determine how best to store data securely and ensure it cannot be viewed by anyone who is unauthorised to do so.

CONSENT

It is good practice to obtain informed consent from everyone who will be taking part in your research and it is likely this will be a requirement of your ethical approval. A common approach is to ask respondents to read, understand and sign an *informed consent form* that outlines what is being asked of them and requires all participants to sign to indicate that they are happy to proceed. Your organisation can further advise you and likely provide you with appropriate templates.

You must also ensure you comply with any relevant data protection legislation in your jurisdiction. In the UK the relevant laws are the UK GDPR/Data Protection Act 2018 legislation. This places strict requirements on organisations (known as *data controllers*) to protect personal data and to have a *lawful basis for processing* data, which includes research data if it is collected from individuals. Your data governance or data protection team can help you understand what is required of you, but you will typically need informed consent from respondents to collect their personal data, as well as explicit consent to collect any *special category data* such as racial or ethnic origin, health or sexual orientation. Collecting *criminal offence* data also carries additional requirements, so ensure you speak to your data governance team in good time.

DO NO HARM

Respondents should not be in a position where they are harmed or may potentially be harmed as a result of participating in your research. This includes physical harm and psychological harm. As researchers we mitigate these by ensuring that participation in our research is voluntary (respondents should be able to refuse to participate) and that respondents can opt out from our research at any time without penalty (they can *withdraw* from the research), and they should not be negatively affected regardless of whether they choose to participate or not participate.

REFLECTIVE PRACTICE 5.4

LEVEL 4

- Why is it important to carry out our research in an ethical manner?

- What could be the consequences for ourselves, our respondents or our organisations if we behave unethically?

WRITING UP YOUR RESEARCH

Having planned, gathered and analysed your data, the final task is to write up your research. Communicating your results is important so that others can learn from your work. Even if you find an intervention to be ineffective you should still share this information, otherwise others might repeat the work you have already done unnecessarily. Chapter 6 describes how to write up your findings and how to publish them.

CONCLUSION

This chapter looked at why and how you might carry out your own research (or at least ask someone else to carry out the research for you). It is important that there is new research and it should offer insight into a particular problem or response to ensure the research is focused. The basic types of research methods available were outlined, including how you can decide which is most appropriate for your needs, and how to ensure you carry out your research ethically and to a high standard. We demonstrated that research is about using skills and knowledge you likely already have and applying them in a systematic way to make practical decisions.

SUMMARY OF KEY CONCEPTS

This chapter has discussed some of the following key concepts.

⚙ **Research questions:** the three to five broad questions that frame your research project overall. These are *not* the questions you ask in an interview or questionnaire.

⚙ **Research methodologies:** these are the two approaches to research (qualitative and quantitative) that allow you to understand different aspects of a problem.

⚙ **Validity and reliability:** indicators of the quality of the data you obtain.

⚙ **Research ethics:** the moral and legal requirements we should meet as police officers and researchers to protect our respondents, ourselves and our organisations.

CHECK YOUR KNOWLEDGE

1. When should you carry out your own research?

2. Why are research questions important to the outcome of your research?

3. What are the two main methodologies (research approaches) you might use?

4. Why are research ethics important to consider?

5. How could you share the results of your research? Why is this important?

FURTHER READING

BOOKS AND BOOK CHAPTERS

Bryman, A (2008) *Social Research Methods*. 3rd ed. Oxford: Oxford University Press.
This is one of the most accessible and most comprehensive textbooks when it comes to
research methods. It covers all aspects of qualitative and quantitative research, and thus
is a useful text to have to hand for a range of projects. Any recent edition will be helpful.

Gilbert, N and Stoneman, P (eds) (2015) *Researching Social Life*. 4th ed. London: Sage.
This edited collection brings together chapters on all aspects of designing a research
project, with each chapter written by a specialist in that particular aspect of social
research. Still accessible but more in-depth than Bryman.

Scott, D (2018) The Politics and Ethics of Criminological Research. In Davies, P and
Francis, P (eds) *Doing Criminological Research*. 3rd ed. Thousand Oaks, CA: Sage.
Scott's book chapter is a good introduction to political and ethical concerns that you
should be aware of as a researcher.

WEBSITES

British Society of Criminology (2015) Statement of Ethics. [online] Available at: www.
britsoccrim.org/ethics (accessed 15 January 2022).
The British Society of Criminology's Statement of Ethics is also an excellent resource.

College of Policing (2021) 'How to' Research Guides. [online] Available at: https://
whatworks.college.police.uk/Support/Pages/Research-guidance.aspx (accessed
15 January 2022).
The College of Policing *What Works* website has a number of useful resources to help with
research projects. The *logic model* is a good starting point in particular.

Social Research Association (2021) Research Ethics Guidance. [online] Available at: https://
the-sra.org.uk/SRA/Ethics/Research-ethics-guidance/SRA/Ethics/Research-Ethics-Guidance.
aspx (accessed 15 January 2022).
The Social Research Association's ethical guidance is an excellent resource to further
develop your understanding of ethical considerations in research.

CHAPTER 6
USING EVIDENCE TO DEVELOP PRACTICE

LEARNING OBJECTIVES

AFTER READING THIS CHAPTER YOU WILL BE ABLE TO:

- consolidate information and data gathered;

- understand how to structure a research report or research dissertation;

- apply this knowledge to produce your own research output;

- identify to whom and where to present or publish your findings;

- adapt your report and findings to meet the requirements of different audiences.

INTRODUCTION

In previous chapters we showed you how to gather, analyse and summarise key data and information, and this takes a lot of time and effort. Rather than the results of that effort gathering dust and never being used, this chapter guides you through the process of writing up and presenting research so that it can be used by other practitioners. Ultimately, the purpose of all this effort is to inform and develop evidence-based practice.

In this chapter we cover both written reports and presentations (or briefings). These are common ways of sharing the results of your research with academic and practitioner audiences. In particular, we describe how to write up research into a suitable report or dissertation format; how to prepare for and give a presentation or briefing; and how to ensure you adjust your material to the needs of different audiences. Throughout we illustrate these with case studies and examples, drawing out good practice and some common issues with sharing research findings. We begin by describing how a research report or dissertation should be structured and what it should contain.

STRUCTURE OF WRITTEN REPORTS

The vast majority of research projects, whether these are practitioner-based or academic dissertations, will involve writing up your findings into a written report format, even if you subsequently produce additional material or give presentations or briefings about your research. If you are a practitioner writing a report then it ensures your findings are available at any time to any potential readers without your input. If you are an academic student writing a dissertation, it is the most common form of assessment for a research project.

Irrespective of whether you are writing a report or dissertation, the structure and format of either are very similar and include broadly the same content, with some minor differences that we will point out. Common sections are:

- title page;

- acknowledgements;

- abstract or executive summary;

- contents page;

- glossary;

- introduction;

- literature review;

- methods;

- results;

- discussion and conclusions;

- bibliography;

- appendices.

TITLE PAGE

Your title page should include, as the name suggests, a succinct title for your research. Good titles will describe the focus of your study and relevant keywords so that readers can quickly determine if your report is relevant to them. An example of a good title might be 'Effectiveness of ignition interlocks for preventing alcohol-impaired driving and alcohol-related crashes' (Elder et al, 2011). From the title it is clear that the study is trying to assess how effective ignition interlocks (car breathalyser locks) are at reducing alcohol-impaired driving and alcohol-related crashes (drink driving). The title is good because there is enough information in just the title for the reader to make an informed decision about how relevant the study is to their needs. Consider an alternative title, 'Reducing drink driving'. There is still some information in the title but it is arguably not descriptive enough for the reader to find using common search techniques.

If you are producing a dissertation you should check with your tutors or institution whether they require particular information. This might include:

- student number or ID;

- programme and/or module of study;

- supervisor;

- date of submission;

- word count;

- statement of compliance.

If you are producing a report, especially for publication, you will instead likely need to include bibliographical information, such as:

- author names and affiliations;

- place of publication, or name of the organisation publishing the research;

- commissioning body, if different from the publisher;

- date of publication;

- identifier, such as a Digital Object Identifier (DOI) or ISBN;

- copyright and licensing information.

You should check with your research office or similar in your organisation for specific advice.

ACKNOWLEDGEMENTS

This section should acknowledge any individuals, groups or organisations that played an instrumental role in the successful completion of your report. Typically this will mean:

- funders, if your research is funded;

- organisations that allowed access for your research;

- individuals or groups that helped with recruitment, such as by providing introductions;

- individuals who provided substantive feedback on the report, but who are not an author;

- your respondents.

If you are completing a dissertation it is also common (but not necessary) for students to thank:

- family, friends or partners who helped or offered support;

- supervisors;

- any other individuals who have helped you, for example with proofreading.

ABSTRACT OR EXECUTIVE SUMMARY

The abstract and executive summary are very similar in structure and purpose, where 'abstract' tends to be common in academic writing while 'executive summary' tends to be common in reports. Both essentially perform the same purpose of condensing the research into an easily consumable format, typically no more than one or two pages.

The abstract or executive summary should contain enough information that a reader could understand the main findings of your research without having to read the whole document. Typically this is done by providing only cursory information about methods and sampling, and concentrating on high-level results.

Unstructured executive summaries or abstracts are common and do not use any sub-headings (ie in essay form). Structured abstracts are those that use sub-headings that mirror the wider report (introduction, methods, results, conclusions). Structured abstracts are common in some disciplines and are becoming more common in policing; the *Cambridge Journal of Evidence-Based Policing*, for example, makes extensive use of structured abstracts in its articles. Check with your organisation or institution to see if they have particular requirements.

CONTENTS PAGE

You should provide a contents page which lists the main sections or headings of your report with their respective page numbers. This becomes more important the longer your report becomes.

If you are using Microsoft Word (or other similar word processing software) you can assign your headings an appropriate style, such as 'Heading 1' for top-level heading, 'Heading 2' for sub-headings, and so on. You can then insert a table of contents automatically from the 'References' tab of the ribbon. You can update your table of contents by clicking on the table and selecting 'Update table'. Your word processor's help function, or an internet search, can provide more information on these steps if required.

GLOSSARY

The first time you use an acronym or abbreviation in your report, it is convention to write the full term and then provide the shorter term in brackets. Each subsequent time you refer to the term you can simply use the shortened version. For example, you might discuss anti-social behaviour (ASB) as part of your research, and go on to discuss how ASB is the most common event recorded by police in many cities of the UK. If you use lots of acronyms, abbreviations or subject-specific terms, you might want to consider adding a glossary for quick reference for your readers. These should be listed in alphabetical order and an example is given in Table 6.1.

Table 6.1 Example glossary with acronyms/abbreviations and definitions

Acronym	Definition
ASB	Anti-social behaviour
PACE	Police and Criminal Evidence Act (1984)

INTRODUCTION

Your introduction sets the scene for your report and should generally include:

- a summary of what your research is going to be about;

- why it is important or significant – why this research, and why now?

- what new contribution it makes. Is it an under-researched area? Is there general research that you apply in a local or specific context? Does it summarise existing research in a new way?

- your research questions. You should state these explicitly.

LITERATURE REVIEW

Once you've set the scene with your introduction, your literature review should provide your reader with essential information to understand your research and its current context. This would typically include:

- a summary of existing related research studies, and what their strengths and weaknesses (gaps) are overall;

- how your research complements or fits in this wider research;

- key terms or terminology readers should be aware of to understand the topic.

Your literature review will need to include relevant publications and reports produced by organisations such as the Home Office, National Police Chiefs Council and the College of Policing. It should also include relevant academic research, which can be obtained by searching your institution's library or the National Police Library. It is important to include such material because it demonstrates your knowledge of the subject matter and increases confidence in your findings.

Your reader should be able to read your literature review section and understand everything they need to (even if it's only at a basic level) about your topic to properly assess your work. Refer back to Chapters 3 and 4 for further help in conducting a literature review.

METHODS

Your methods section should describe *how* you went about your study. The aim is to provide enough detail that someone else (or you, in a year's time when you've forgotten what you did) could replicate your study exactly as you produced it. The methods section tends to be fairly descriptive, and could perhaps be thought of as the equivalent to the steps involved in a cooking recipe.

You should start by stating whether you used a qualitative, quantitative or mixed-methods approach, and why this was the most appropriate choice to answer your research questions. If one or more of your research questions required different, separate approaches, then it is okay to be explicit about which approach you adopted for each research question and why.

You should then go on to state which specific method or methods you used. If you carried out qualitative primary research, did you use interviews, focus groups or a different method? If instead you gathered quantitative data, was this through an online survey, face-to-face survey or something else?

You should also describe here how you recruited respondents for your study: What was the population from which you drew your sample? How did you sample (recruit) respondents from your population? And what limitations are there with this sampling technique? Refer back to Chapter 5 for help with sampling.

You must ensure you provide sufficient detail; for example, it is not enough to say 'I posted an advert on social media'. You should include details of which social media platform or platforms you used and describe how you approached people on that platform.

- Did you post a general invitation to connections (friends) or post in a group with a specific interest?

- Who is or can be a member of that group (is it open for all to join, or are there restrictions on who can join that group)?

- Is it based on location or an interest or a group already known to each other (for example, members of a university course)?

You should state when you sent out the invitation and any reminders and how many respondents replied at each stage. You should also describe how respondents could participate. Increasingly this is mediated by online digital tools such as Microsoft Forms or Google Forms, specialist software such as Qualtrics, or online interviews or focus groups using group chat software. However, you may have used traditional techniques such as face-to-face meetings or paper surveys. Either way, it is important to make this clear and unambiguous.

If you have analysed secondary data you will need to write this up slightly differently, but the underlying principles are the same. You should describe where your data was obtained from and provide a bibliographical reference. Data sources such as the UK Data Service provide bibliographical citations with their data sets that you should include. Ensure you record (and provide) the date you downloaded the data. Although you did not do the sampling and recruiting yourself, you should nevertheless describe how respondents were recruited for the data set and what the sampling method used by the original data collectors was. This is important because it affects how representative the data is and what population it represents. See Chapter 5 for more information on representative sampling.

If your method is instead a systematic literature review, we strongly encourage you to follow the PRISMA guidelines (PRISMA, 2021) for reporting systematic literature reviews or meta-analyses. PRISMA is written with a wider audience than policing in mind (and typically is used for medical systematic reviews) so not all steps will be relevant to your own report, and you should use your judgement before including irrelevant information. Nevertheless, we suggest using this approach because it is standardised and evidence-based, and research partners such as the NHS will be familiar with it. You should seek advice, for example from your academic supervisor or your research team, if you are unsure on how to proceed with this.

Whether you have gathered primary data, used secondary data, carried out a systematic literature review, or a combination of these approaches, you should describe how you analysed the data or information you collected. If you are working with primarily qualitative data, it is likely you will be reviewing this for themes, perhaps using content analysis or discourse analysis. Quantitative data will require a different approach and will likely require some exploratory analysis and some statistical analysis. A systematic literature review might be a narrative review or you might perform a meta-analysis if the data you have gathered supports this.

Finally, it is helpful to conclude by stating why you chose these methods or approaches over others. If other methods could have been used it might be helpful to discuss why you settled on your chosen approach, which might be for practical reasons such as time or cost, and if other approaches were not appropriate you should explain this. You should aim to tie back your methods to your research question and demonstrate to the reader that these match well and, ultimately, produce valid conclusions that can be trusted.

RESULTS

Your results and discussion section should summarise what you found from your study and offer some analysis as to why or how you found these results. The aim of the results chapter is to identify patterns and reasons (if possible) for those patterns. A results chapter will typically start with simple analyses of each variable or theme individually and then build up to identifying patterns between variables or themes. If you are writing your dissertation, this is perhaps the easiest chapter in which to demonstrate critical thinking skills and boost your mark significantly, so don't neglect it.

Your results chapter should usually include the following aspects.

- A systematic summary of each important individual variable (quantitative) or theme (qualitative).

- An analysis of multiple themes and/or variables, with the aim of describing how they relate to each other.

- If you can, insight as to *why* you think there is a relationship between variables or themes. You can do this by referring to your data and linking it back to relevant reading in your literature review.

- A short summary of what you found overall.

For example, if you are researching the link between victimisation of crime and ethnicity, you will have collected some measures about your respondents' ethnic group and if they had been a victim of crime. You may have also collected other demographic information about your respondents, and you might have broken down victimisation into different crime types. We recommend in this example that your results chapter should include a summary and short discussion of each variable or theme (ethnic group, victimisation). This should then be followed up by analysis of both variables together.

- What proportion of respondents from different ethnic groups have been victims of crime?

- Are there any patterns you can identify (are people from different ethnic groups more or less likely to have been a victim of crime)?

- Can you offer any explanations as to *why* this is the case? You should draw on your analysis and link it back to your literature review to do this convincingly.

You may wish to include tables and, if appropriate, charts or other figures in your results section. These can be very useful to illustrate relationships between variables or themes.

You should use them sparingly, though. Make a conscious and deliberate choice about which figures to include and which points you wish to highlight with them. Don't just include tables or figures of every variable as this can be very distracting for the reader.

We would strongly encourage you to report negative findings, and not be tempted to dismiss them as not useful to other researchers or practitioners. Instead, knowing what doesn't work can be at least as useful as knowing what does work, as it can prevent time and money being spent on something that has already been tested and found to be ineffective. See the evidence-based policing box for an example.

EVIDENCE-BASED POLICING

THE IMPORTANCE OF REPORTING NEGATIVE FINDINGS

It can be tempting to disregard negative findings and not publish them, overlooking them as unimportant or unlikely to be of interest. On the contrary, publishing negative findings can be extremely valuable as it prevents others from repeating the same research, only to also find it does not work. Take Cumberbatch and Barnes (2018). In this paper the authors use a randomised control trial to test if sending a 'warning' (that is, a reminder or nudge) of court dates to victims and witnesses is effective in reducing non-attendance. They determine it is not effective, and non-attendance was similar in both the treatment and control groups. By publishing their research they potentially prevent others from repeating the research, only for them to also find this approach does not work. Just because your research does not find what you set out to, it does not mean that it is not valuable; quite the opposite in fact.

Having reviewed each variable or theme and reviewed important associations between them, it is important to conclude your results chapter with a summary of the main finding or findings overall. You may have identified and discussed several variables or themes that have associations but in concluding this chapter it is important to review the overall picture for your readers.

DISCUSSION AND CONCLUSION

The final chapter of your dissertation or report is the conclusion, sometimes called the discussion and conclusion. It is for recapping what you have written so far, wrapping up your work and analyses, and identifying to the reader what should happen next.

You should begin your conclusion chapter by recapping what your original research questions are and why they needed studying. Next you should outline the method or methods you used and why these were suited to answering your research questions. This might only be one paragraph to remind the reader of these points.

At this stage you should also remind readers of the limitations of your chosen method or sampling strategy and, crucially, how these might affect how they should interpret your results. For example, a convenience sample might offer valuable insight into a phenomenon or group, but will not necessarily be representative of that group. In this instance, the reader (and the writer) should be careful to avoid stating that the results reflect the opinions or experiences of the whole population.

Next, briefly recap the results you found as outlined in your results and analysis chapter. Again, this need only be a paragraph or two with the aim of briefly reminding the reader of your key findings.

The only 'new' information your conclusion should contain is to describe why your results are important and who they might be important to, and to identify what the next steps might be. Having done all this work, after which you will be somewhat of an expert in the subject, you should suggest what you think the next important steps are for this topic. There might be changes in policy or procedure that need implementing to improve outcomes. You might have found that further research is needed to understand it better or understand different aspects of the topic. If this is the case you should state this, but be specific about exactly what policy or procedure changes, or further research, you think are required. See the policing spotlight box for an example of policy recommendations made as a result of the research.

POLICING SPOTLIGHT

Ramiz et al (2020) is a qualitative study of modern slavery on cannabis farms. They identify modern slavery as a significant issue, compounded by the fact that investigation and support by police is inconsistent, and often those who are victimised are not identified as such. The authors therefore recommend three main policy improvements: investigate the presence of modern slavery by soliciting accounts from growers (who are often bound by threats of violence to them or their families); proactively address abusers; and more comprehensive training for uniformed first response officers.

The recommendations made by the authors are aimed at improving the overall police response to investigating modern slavery, and as such it is appropriate that they are not focused on specific policies or procedures, but instead are general in scope and detail to help identify the change that is required.

BIBLIOGRAPHY

Your bibliography is an alphabetical list of all publications you have referred to or cited within your dissertation. It should be included at the end of the main body of your dissertation or report, immediately after the conclusion but before the appendices. The 'Harvard' referencing style tends to be the most commonly used in the social sciences and is most likely the style you should adopt, although you should check with your publisher or dissertation module leader if they require a different style (for example, APA or footnotes). Your university's library will have resources you can refer to for help with correct referencing.

APPENDICES

Your appendices should include any supplementary information that is useful for reference, but not essential to understanding the dissertation. These might include any one or more of the following:

- your approval from your ethics application or ethics board for your research;

- approvals or agreements from other organisations (if applicable);

- a blank copy of (if applicable): your invitation letter to respondents to participate in your research; your participant information sheet; your informed consent form and/ or privacy notice; and your debriefing sheet;

- a blank copy of your survey questions, interview schedule or other data collection instrument;

- you may also wish to include supplementary tables, charts or figures that you did not include in the results section, but that might be useful to readers, for example for comparison purposes.

Now that we have reviewed the main sections a research report or dissertation should contain, reflective practice activity 6.1 will help you consider why a standard approach is useful and if there are occasions when you should deviate from this.

REFLECTIVE PRACTICE 6.1

LEVEL 6

Why do you think it is important to present your research in a standard format, with a standard structure?

a) Why is it useful for you, the writer?

b) Why is it helpful for the reader?

c) When might it be appropriate to use a different structure?

Sample answers to these questions are provided at the end of the book.

APPROPRIATE WRITING STYLE

When writing a report or dissertation for a professional or academic audience you are encouraged to use objective and tentative language, and to use evidence to support your arguments. This means that instead of asserting a point as a fact you should soften your language and present your ideas supported by your evidence. Consider the difference between the following sentences.

* Knife crime *was* fuelled by a gang culture.

* The evidence *suggests* that a gang culture was responsible for knife crime.

See how the language has been 'softened' in the second sentence. It still states essentially the same information, which is that a gang culture is linked to knife crime, but it states it in such a way that there is still room for other factors or causes to be responsible for the knife crime.

This is because it can be very difficult to establish exact causes of issues such as knife crime, which are complex and likely the result of more than one cause. As academics or researchers, we therefore say that there is evidence to support the assertion without over-stating the strength of it. Consider using words like 'appears', 'indicates', 'tends to support', 'could', 'might', 'possibly', 'likely', and so on. This can help to demonstrate that you are keeping a critical mind with regard to your own research too.

You will discover as you go through your studies that there are lots of different ways of looking at any one problem and lots of different ways of interpreting the information. You will be presenting one particular interpretation. Therefore, it is important that you use tentative language to present your research as an idea, open for debate, rather than as a factual claim to the truth.

WHERE TO PUBLISH

If you are looking to publish your work (and you should!) there are a number of possible avenues available to you, and you should consider which is the most appropriate approach. Some of the more common options are:

- within your own constabulary;

- the College of Policing;

- professional publications;

- research organisations and other non-governmental organisations;

- peer-reviewed journals.

We now explore each of these in more detail.

WITHIN YOUR OWN CONSTABULARY

Individual police constabularies might have their own internal 'libraries' where you can publish and share research. Your constabulary might also have an Evidenced-based Policing Board or similar where you might share your research. You might also share your research on your constabulary's intranet. In these cases, you should speak to your research team, training department or line manager for assistance.

If you publish internally, remember that individuals outside of the constabulary will not be able to see your research. This might be desirable if, for example, your research contains sensitive material; in such cases, you might want to consider publishing a 'full' version internally but still making available a 'public' version if possible. See Chapter 3, particularly Resource Pillar 5 on page 53, for further advice.

THE COLLEGE OF POLICING

The College of Policing routinely publish research carried out at Master's level and above, or that written by professionals in the *Policing and Crime Reduction Research Map*. An internet search for 'college of policing and crime reduction research map' will return the relevant page, or can be accessed at https://whatworks.college.police.uk/Research/Resea rch-Map/Pages/Research-Map.aspx (accessed 25 November 2021). You can register your research with this page for other practitioners to see.

The College of Policing also publish articles in *Going Equipped*, which is a series of articles written by police officers and staff, and therefore may be suitable for less formal publications of your research. Search 'college of policing going equipped' for these articles.

Finally, the College of Policing have an 'evidence champions network' of police officers and staff members who are involved in EBP within their constabulary. You can find and contact your relevant evidence champion through the *Evidence Champions Network* page: https://whatworks.college.police.uk/Support/Pages/epc.aspx (accessed 25 November 2021).

PROFESSIONAL PUBLICATIONS

There are a number of professional publications and magazines that may be appropriate to publish in, depending on your requirements. For example, you may choose to publish your research report with the College of Policing and write a shorter piece to send to one or more professional publications that direct readers to the full findings. Examples include:

* *National Police Chiefs' Council*, for example in their 'Latest News';

* *POLICE* magazine from the Police Federation;

* *Policing Insight*;

* *Police Professional.*

RESEARCH ORGANISATIONS AND OTHER NGOs

Depending on the focus of your research there may also be non-governmental organisations interested in publishing your work. These are often, but not always, aligned to universities involved in criminal justice research. Examples include: UCL Jill Dando Institute of Security and Crime Science; CENTRIC at Sheffield Hallam University; Institute for Crime & Justice Policy Research; and the Centre for Crime and Justice Studies.

PEER-REVIEWED JOURNALS

Finally, a peer-reviewed academic journal might be the most appropriate outlet to publish your research. Journals such as the *Cambridge Journal of Evidence-Based Policing, Crime Prevention and Community Safety, Police Practice and Research*, or a more specialist journal if appropriate, might be worth considering. Each journal will have slightly different requirements for submitting your research and you should check their website. If you need advice you should ask your research team, or the National Police Library may also be able to recommend suitable journals.

Having looked in more detail at a number of publication options, you might be thinking where you might publish your own research. Reflective practice activity 6.2 guides you through the process of selecting a suitable outlet.

REFLECTIVE PRACTICE 6.2

LEVEL 6

If you have a research project that is either complete, near completion or in progress, consider where you might meaningfully publish the results.

a) Is the format you are currently writing suitable for publication? If not, can it be modified so that it is?

b) Make a shortlist of suitable publishers or organisations that you could approach to publish your research. You might consider general policing publications or a more specific outlet if your research is on a focused topic.

c) Do you need to contact organisations to ask if they would be interested in publishing your research? Sometimes it can be easier to get your research published if you already have an existing relationship with suitable organisations.

Sample answers to these questions are provided at the end of the book

PREPARING A PRESENTATION OF YOUR RESEARCH

If you are asked to give an oral presentation of your research or your research findings this might be a daunting prospect, but you should remember that this is *your research* and *you* are an expert in it. That's not to say that you can't also learn from participants, but they will be interested to hear what *your research* has found and what they should do.

There are also some practical steps you can take to improve your presentation skills and increase your confidence. Remember to write down key information such as the date, time and location you will be giving the presentation. You can also ask the person who invited you to present about the likely audience: this might help you to tweak your presentation accordingly. For example, if you are addressing a neighbourhood policing team there might be adjustments you can make to make your presentation relevant to the neighbourhood or neighbourhoods they police.

Plan your presentation using headings and bullet points to ensure you do not miss any vital information. We recommend against writing down verbatim what you wish to say as you are not giving a speech and it can be difficult to make your presentation engaging if you are reading from a script. Instead, we suggest making yourself some prompt cards with short notes to remind yourself of the point you wish to discuss. This can help your presentation to be more natural, which is easier to make engaging for your audience.

If you wish to use PowerPoint or similar presentation software, use it sparingly. We advise against writing out everything you wish to say. Instead, use bullet points and a larger font so that participants can skim the points but can continue to pay attention to what you are saying. Of course, presentation software is excellent for sharing images such as tables, maps or charts. See Leicester (2017), especially Chapter 9, for more guidance in producing an effective presentation.

PREPARING MATERIALS FOR A PRACTITIONER AUDIENCE

In addition to your research report or publication, you should also consider how to ensure the findings from your research reach a wider audience, to actually influence policy or practice. While a research report should be available so interested parties can scrutinise it, a series of practical guidelines will have far more reach and utility, and are more likely to be adopted.

While the research report will contain all the necessary detail used to produce the research, the guidance material will typically only contain information on what to do, when to do it and how to do it. This helps keep the quantity of content and reading down so that it is easily understood, but can of course link to and refer to the wider research when appropriate. Refer to the evidence-based policing box below for an example of preparing research for a practitioner audience.

EVIDENCE-BASED POLICING

OBTAINING INITIAL ACCOUNTS

The College of Policing have recently published guidance on obtaining initial accounts (College of Policing, 2019c). The guidance is evidence-based, drawing on a 'rapid evidence assessment' (Finn et al, 2019), but is presented in a much more accessible format for practitioners.

In the guidance, individual recommendations are presented in a summary table. This states the recommendation and identifies if empirical (research) evidence and/or practitioner evidence is available, and what the strength of that evidence is (good, moderate or limited). In this way, readers can quickly understand what they should do and how to obtain the further evidence and research if they wish.

CONCLUSION

In this chapter we have covered how to effectively share your results and findings with colleagues and other practitioners, in the form of a written report, a presentation (or briefing) and guidance for a practitioner audience. We have also considered how to ensure you adjust your material to the needs of different audiences. We have examined case studies and examples that have highlighted good practice and some common issues with sharing research findings. You now have the tools to take this knowledge to share your own findings with your colleagues for the benefit of policing.

SUMMARY OF KEY CONCEPTS

This chapter has discussed some of the following key concepts.

The structure of a dissertation or research report: we have considered how to write up your research using a common structure that is used widely, both within and beyond the discipline that readers will likely be familiar with.

Publishing: we have provided some suggestions as to where you should publish your research. This will depend on the nature and style of your research, which you will need to consider when deciding on a suitable outlet. Nevertheless, we encourage you to publish your research *somewhere* so that it can be reviewed and scrutinised by other practitioners.

Presenting: sometimes you might be asked (or offer) to provide an oral presentation of your research. Remember that you are the expert in your research.

Producing guidance or materials for practitioners: this can be an effective way to ensure your recommendations reach a wider audience. Remember to report only the findings and recommendations; you can always refer back to the wider research if necessary.

CHECK YOUR KNOWLEDGE

1. Why is it important to publish your research?

2. Should you always publish your work? Are there times when publishing is not advised? Is there anything you can do to mitigate this?

3. How can you make the findings of your research accessible to a practitioner audience?

4. Should you publish negative findings? Why or why not?

5. Can you work with other individuals or organisations to further publicise your work?

FURTHER READING

BOOKS AND BOOK CHAPTERS

Booth, A, Sutton, A and Papaioannou, D (2016) *Systematic Approaches to a Successful Literature Review*. 2nd ed. Los Angeles: Sage.
If you wish to complete a systematic literature review, we recommend the above book to guide you through the process.

Bottomley, J, Pryjmachuk, S and Wright, M (2020) *Academic Writing and Referencing for your Policing Degree*. St Albans: Critical Publishing.
This book from the *Critical Study Skills for Policing* series might be helpful with academic writing skills, building and developing your argument, and using sources effectively.

Evergreen, S D H (2017) *Effective Data Visualization: The Right Chart for the Right Data*. Los Angeles: Sage.
This book provides help with producing effective and correct charts, figures and graphs.

McMillan, K and Weyers, J (2011) *How to Write Dissertations & Project Reports*. Harlow: Pearson.
The above book discusses how to write a research report or dissertation, in particular the chapter 'Writing a first draft'.

WEBSITES

College of Policing (2021) Study Skills Toolkit. [online] Available at: https://leadership.coll ege.police.uk/course/view.php?id=37 (accessed 15 January 2022).
The College of Policing have several courses and toolkits that may be of use, especially the *Study Skills Toolkit* (requires registration).

PRISMA (2021) *Transparent Reporting of Systematic Reviews and Meta-Analyses*. [online] Available at: www.prisma-statement.org/ (accessed 15 January 2022).
If you wish to produce a systematic literature review you should follow the PRISMA guidance.

SAMPLE ANSWERS

CHAPTER 1

REFLECTIVE PRACTICE 1.1

Policing has sometimes been seen as a craft that can only be learned through experience and time *on the job*. Policing culture (the way things are done around here) can be passed through the generations from more experienced to less experienced officers, creating a way of thinking and acting that can be resistant to change. Next time you are in the workplace, revisit this exercise and really start to explore where your knowledge comes from and why you are doing things the way you do. Start to really explore what actually underpins your practice and this will also help you to develop as a reflective practitioner.

CRITICAL THINKING ACTIVITY 1.1

a) You should be basing your decisions on the most reliable data you can obtain and also on the fullest data set that you can proportionately gather. Therefore, in this scenario using the analyst's information would be the recommended option.

b) Your own experience is limited to only a few examples. The analyst has oversight of many incidents and can provide a fuller and more detailed and complete analysis. The analyst's product allows you to target the patrol strategy at the times and locations most likely to make a difference. It provides an auditable trail and clear rationale to support your decision-making about deployment of resources.

CRITICAL THINKING ACTIVITY 1.2

a) Are you hoping to prevent further burglaries? Are you hoping to capture the offender? Are you hoping to gather intelligence to allow you to further the investigation? Are you hoping to provide public reassurance? Each of these needs careful consideration.

b) You need to consider any legal implications of using the drone. Use of drones as a surveillance tool is subject to rules and guidelines in much the same way as CCTV. Some of the areas you would need to explore would be compliance with Civil Aviation Authority rules, the Surveillance Camera Code of Practice, Protection of Freedoms Act 2012, European Court of Human Rights, Regulation of Investigatory Powers Act 2000, Data Protection Act 2018, and the Police Code of Ethics. You would also need to consider a privacy impact assessment and ensure that you had procedures in place in case of any complaints about the use of the drone. You would need to explore if there are any policies or guidance documents on the use of drones that you should follow and also what training the drone pilot has completed.

c) Would your drone be deployed overtly or covertly? Patrols in a marked police car may act as a visible deterrent to support crime prevention and may also raise public reassurance. Would a drone be able to achieve this? Would you consider publicising the use of the drone and what effect might this have? If the outcome you hope to achieve is to arrest the offender, then what plans do you have in place if the drone operator sees a burglary in progress? Is a drone more effective or less effective than visible police patrols? Have any other police forces used a drone in this way and what were their experiences? How might the public react to this approach? These are just some of the wider considerations, but you can probably already see that deployment of a drone requires careful consideration to protect the rights of the public, protect the integrity of any material gathered and ensure resources are being used to the best effect.

CHAPTER 2

CRITICAL THINKING ACTIVITY 2.1

For either question, you may have included words such as: exploring; examining; questioning; uncovering; searching; probing; testing; analysing; systematic; orderly; organised; fair; impartial; objective; thorough; detailed.

CRITICAL THINKING ACTIVITY 2.2

You may have included questions like these.

a) Who is Nicky Seville? Who is the radio broadcaster?

b) What political alliance does Nicky Seville have? What evidence is there that visible patrols decrease burglaries? What is the actual number of burglaries?

c) Why are the burglary rates rising? Why is there a perception that police visibility decreases crime?

d) Where are the burglary statistics drawn from? Where are the burglary rates rising specifically?

e) When did police numbers decrease and when did the burglary rates increase?

f) How else could burglaries be tackled? How many police are patrolling now compared to 12 months ago and 15 years ago?

CRITICAL THINKING ACTIVITY 2.3

a) Evidence of bias may be seen in the following areas:

- he has a preconceived idea about what he will find;

- the aim of his research is to establish the advantages of working from home;

- he is only searching for literature that supports his pre-existing belief;

- he is selecting participants that feel the same way he does;

- he is only reporting the benefits of working from home.

b) In order to demonstrate a lack of bias he could:

- change his aim to ensure he is exploring the advantages and disadvantages of working from home;

- search for, and use, literature that explores different perspectives on working from home;

- use a recognised sampling strategy to ensure a range of participants are selected with more chance of diverse views;

- report his participants' interviews accurately, reflecting both the advantages and disadvantages of working from home;

- keep a reflective diary.

CHAPTER 3

CRITICAL THINKING ACTIVITY 3.1

As you gradually reduced the parameters of your search you should have found fewer 'hits' each time until the final search in speech marks, which provided one answer. This might be too specific but now you understand the way search engines function, you can tailor your search strategy to suit your requirements.

CRITICAL THINKING ACTIVITY 3.2

a) The most accurate information will be on the Home Office website.

b) Search for the Home Office webpage using www.gov.uk. Then scroll down and find the research at the Home Office tab. Find the policing research and analysis tab, then find the research you require.

Because the www.gov.uk site is well organised, you can use this same easy step guide to finding research on the majority of government websites.

CRITICAL THINKING ACTIVITY 3.3

Our strategy would be to use the National Crime Agency website (www.nationalcrimeagency. gov.uk). From the home page use the search box at the top right, enter your search terms and start browsing the available information. You should be able to find the strategic threat assessment document on the site plus much more information about serious and organised crime.

CHAPTER 4

CRITICAL THINKING ACTIVITY 4.1

You may have thought about questions such as:

* why was the battle was fought?

* whether there were any political or social reasons for the battle;

* whether any factors prior to the battle influenced its outcome;

* whether any tactical errors on the part of the Saxons contributed to a Norman victory;

* whether there was a difference in armaments between the two sides.

CRITICAL THINKING ACTIVITY 4.2

Remember there is no right or wrong and you may have chosen to pick out the following trigger words:

> *freight (eg, mail parcels, medicines, fire extinguishing material, flyers, etc) and sensors (eg, cameras, sniffers, meteorological sensors, etc). Applications of payloads; perform a flight; wireless communication with a pilot on the ground. Communication; frequency spectrum is required. type of drone, the flight characteristics; international coordination*

The underlined words are the important parts of the text, and you can go on to search other literature for the terms and build on the information you have found. Because this is a passage from an article abstract, you now also have a good idea what the article will cover and its relevance to your project.

CRITICAL THINKING ACTIVITY 4.3

You may have thought about questions such as the following.

- Who is the author or source of the information?

- When was the document written or the information provided?

- What was the purpose or objective of the document or information?

- What is the subject and context of the document or information?

- Why was it written and what is its objective, then and now?

- If it is research data (raw or otherwise), how was it collected?

- How is the article or information presented?

- Does it present a balanced view or is it biased?

- What do you think about the article or data?

The source paragraph was taken from this article: Ford, R (2020) Failing Police 'Rumbled' by Weary Public. *The Times*, 7 February. [online] Available at: www.thetimes.co.uk/article/failing-police-rumbled-by-weary-public-7lwvxrdr6 (accessed 15 January 2022).

CRITICAL THINKING ACTIVITY 4.4

Here is a ready-made checklist list of things to check for when evaluating the credibility of an internet information source (Georgetown University, 2021). You may discover other ways which you can add to the list as you conduct research in the future.

- Is the name of the author/creator on the page?

- Are his/her credentials listed (occupation, years of experience, position or education)?

- Is the author qualified to write on the given topic? Why?

- Is there contact information, such as an email address, somewhere on the page?

- Is there a link to a homepage?

- If there is a link to a homepage, is it for an individual or for an organisation?

- If the author is with an organisation, does it appear to support or sponsor the page?

- What does the domain name/URL reveal about the source of the information, if anything?

- If the owner is not identified, what can you tell about the origin of the site from the address?

(Georgetown University, 2021)

REFLECTIVE PRACTICE 4.1

University sites are an excellent example of sites which have a lot of information for prospective students, but the underlying motive is to persuade you to attend their institution. It is the same with business and corporate sites. They may provide information but their ultimate aim is to sell you a product or service. This reflective practice activity is simply a caution to remind you not to take sites at face value, delve deeper and apply the critical thinking skills you have learned to avoid misinformation, bias and inaccuracy in your research endeavours.

ANSWER TO POLICING SPOTLIGHT (PAGE 79)

By applying the strategies available in this chapter, hopefully you have decided to begin by constructing a data table to manage the information you find regarding each burglary. What at first might seem an overwhelming task can actually be managed in quite a simple and effective way.

Any considerations you may think of regarding the information you find, such as contact details for complainants or forensic similarities, can be dealt with in the table. All of the details you require will be in one place. The example below is not exhaustive regarding what you can include in your table, but it should present a clear idea of how easy it is to record bulk information in a clear, precise and systematic way (see below).

Crime number	Date and time	Location	Complainant details	Contact details	Modus operandi (the way the crime was committed)	Forensic evidence

CHAPTER 5

CRITICAL THINKING ACTIVITY 5.1

Your research questions will clearly depend on the problem you choose to tackle. Here are some suggestions relevant to the example of burglary.

1. Has there been an increase in the number of burglaries seen on the estate?

2. What reasons are there for the increase in burglary? Is there a reason or reasons that burglary on this estate has increased?

3. What activities have been tried already? Have they been effective? Can they be modified to be more effective?

4. Do residents on the estate support this response?

CRITICAL THINKING ACTIVITY 5.2

Again, this will depend on your research questions, but generally research questions that ask 'how' or 'why' probably lend themselves to qualitative research. This is because you are asking about the *qualities* of the problem, such as reasons or processes. Qualitative research will help you understand these in greater depth.

Conversely, if your research questions are 'what', when' or 'how many' questions, these will probably lend themselves to quantitative methods. These will help you quantify and count activities such as victimisation or crime.

CRITICAL THINKING ACTIVITY 5.3

This will depend on your own research questions, but taking 'Has there been an increase in the number of burglaries seen on the estate?' (from Critical Thinking Activity 5.1) as an example we might ask something like the following.

1. Are you concerned about the number of burglaries in your area?

2. Would you say you are more or less concerned about burglaries now than you were 12 months ago?

3. Do you think there are more, fewer or about the same number of burglaries in your area than neighbouring areas?

CHAPTER 6

REFLECTIVE PRACTICE 6.1

Using a standard template makes our research accessible and understandable to a wider audience. In particular:

a) it is helpful for you, the writer, because it helps ensure you do not forget to include any relevant or important information, and it provides a ready-made template for you to populate;

b) it is helpful for the reader because they will likely be familiar with this format and will know where to quickly find relevant information. It also means that your research can be scrutinised more easily, which is an important stage in research;

c) sometimes it might be appropriate to use a different format if your research is very different.

REFLECTIVE PRACTICE 6.2

a) If you are not already, consider publishing your research in a standard format, as this can make getting it published easier. If it is not, can you create a version that is?

b) Your shortlist might include general publications or organisations that publish broadly in the discipline of policing, but if your research is particularly focused on a specific area a more specialist outlet might be more appropriate.

c) Just like people, organisations sometimes respond better to offers of publication if they are expecting your research and you already have a relationship with them. You might want to speak to the editor or publications team to see if your research is a good fit, rather than submitting a report 'blind'.

REFERENCES

ACPO and NPIA (2012) *Practice Advice on Core Investigative Doctrine*. Wyboston: NPIA.

Afflerbach, P and Cho, B Y (2010) Determining and Describing Reading Strategies: Internet and Traditional Forms of Reading. In Waters, H S and Schneider, W (eds) *Metacognition, Strategy Use and Instruction*. New York: Guilford Press.

Alpert, G P, Rojeck, J and Hansen, A (2013) *Building Bridges Between Police Researchers and Practitioners: Agents of Change in a Complex World*. US Department of Justice: unpublished.

ASU Center for Problem-Oriented Policing (2021) The SARA Model. [online] Available at: https://popcenter.asu.edu/content/sara-model-0 (accessed 15 January 2022).

Bacon, M, Loftus, B and Rowe, M (2020a) Ethnography and the Evocative World of Policing (Part I). *Policing and Society*, 30(1).

Bacon, M, Loftus, B and Rowe, M (2020b) Ethnography and the Evocative World of Policing (Part II). *Policing and Society*, 30(2).

Baldwin, J (1992) *Video Taping Police Interviews with Suspects: A National Evaluation*. Police Research Series Paper No. 1. London: Home Office Police Department.

Brennan, I (2019) *Victims of Serious Violence in England and Wales, 2011–2017*. London: College of Policing.

British and Irish Legal Information Institute (BAILII) (2021) Search BAILII. [online] Available at: www.bailii.org (accessed 15 January 2022).

Brown, J (1996) Police Research: Some Critical Issues. In Leishman, F, Loveday, B and Savage, S P (eds) *Core Issues in Policing*. London: Longman Group Limited.

Brown, J, Belur, J, Thompson, L, McDowell, A, Hunter, G and May, T (2018) Extending the Remit of Evidence-based Policing. *International Journal of Police Science and Management*: 775017. [online] Available at: http://eprints.lse.ac.uk/86612/7/Brown_Extending%20 the%20remit%20of%20evidence-based%20policing2_.pdf (accessed 15 January 2022).

Bryman, A (2008) *Social Research Methods*. 3rd ed. Oxford: Oxford University Press.

Campbell Collaboration (2021) [online] Available at: www.campbellcollaboration.org/ component/jak2filter/# (accessed 15 January 2022).

Cifas (2021) What is Cifas? [online] Available at: www.cifas.org.uk (accessed 15 January 2022).

College of Policing (2015) 'Scared Straight' Programmes. [online] Available at: https://whatworks.college.police.uk/toolkit/Pages/Intervention.aspx?InterventionID=2 (accessed 15 January 2022).

College of Policing (2016) College and Derbyshire Police Host Evidence-based CPD for Analysts. [online] Available at: https://whatworks.college.police.uk/About/News/Pages/Analyst_day.aspx (accessed 15 January 2022).

College of Policing (2018) About Us: What is APP? [online] Available at: www.app.college.police.uk/about-app (accessed 15 January 2022).

College of Policing (2019a) *Practice Advice: Dealing with Sudden Unexpected Death.* [online] Available at: https://assets.publishing.service.gov.uk/government/uploads/system/uploads/attachment_data/file/922344/Dealing_with_sudden_unexpected_death.pdf (accessed 15 January 2022).

College of Policing (2019b) Investigation: Investigative Interviewing. [online] Available at: www.app.college.police.uk/app-content/investigations/investigative-interviewing (accessed 15 January 2022).

College of Policing (2019c) *Obtaining Initial Accounts from Victims and Witnesses: Guidelines for First Responders*. [online] Available at: https://assets.college.police.uk/s3fs-public/2020-11/Initial_Accounts_Guidelines.pdf (accessed 15 January 2022).

College of Policing (2020a) *Policing Education Qualifications Framework*. [online] Available at: www.college.police.uk/guidance/career-and-learning/policing-education-qualifications-framework-peqf (accessed 15 January 2022).

College of Policing (2020b) Investigation: Investigative Skills. [online] Available at: www.app.college.police.uk/app-content/investigations/introduction/#investigative-skills (accessed 15 January 2022).

College of Policing (2021a) The Policing Evaluation Toolkit. [online] Available at: https://whatworks.college.police.uk/Support/Pages/Evaluation-Toolkit.aspx (accessed 15 January 2022).

College of Policing (2021b) Problem-oriented Policing. [online] Available at: https://whatworks.college.police.uk/toolkit/Pages/Intervention.aspx?InterventionID=47 (accessed 15 January 2022).

College of Policing (2021c) *Introduction to Logic Models*. [online] Available at: https://whatwo rks.college.police.uk/Research/Documents/LogicModel.pdf (accessed 15 January 2022).

College of Policing (2021d) Policing and Crime Reduction Research Map. [online] Available at: https://whatworks.college.police.uk/Research/Research-Map/Pages/Research-Map. aspx (accessed 15 January 2022).

College of Policing (2021e) Research. [online] Available at: https://whatworks.college.pol ice.uk/Research/Pages/default.aspx (accessed 15 January 2022).

College of Policing (2021f) Obtaining Initial Accounts. [online] Available at: www.college. police.uk/guidance/obtaining-initial-accounts (accessed 15 January 2022).

College of Policing (2021g) What is Evidence-based Policing? [online] Available at: https:// whatworks.college.police.uk/About/Pages/What-is-EBP.aspx (accessed 15 January 2022).

College of Policing (2021h) About Us. [online] Available at: https://beta.college.police.uk/ about (accessed 15 January 2022).

College of Policing (2021i) Welcome to the Crime Reduction Toolkit. [online] Available at: https://whatworks.college.police.uk/toolkit/Pages/Welcome.aspx (accessed 15 January 2022).

College of Policing (2021j) Online Resources. [online] Available at: https://whatworks.coll ege.police.uk/Research/overview/Pages/resources.aspx (accessed 15 January 2022).

Courts and Tribunals Judiciary (2021) Structure of the Courts and Tribunal System. [online] Available at: www.judiciary.uk/about-the-judiciary/the-justice-system/court-structure (accessed 15 January 2022).

Crawford, A and Evans, K (eds) (2017) *Crime Prevention and Community Safety*. Oxford: Oxford University Press.

Cumberbatch, J and Barnes, G (2018) This Nudge Was Not Enough: A Randomised Trial of Text Message Reminders of Court Dates to Victims and Witnesses. *Cambridge Journal of Evidence-Based Policing*, 2: 35–51.

Custers, B (ed) (2016) *The Future of Drone Use*. The Hague: TMC Asser Press.

Elder, R, Voas, R, Beirness, D, Shults, R, Sleet, D, Nichols, J and Compton, R (2011) Effectiveness of Ignition Interlocks for Preventing Alcohol-Impaired Driving and Alcohol-Related Crashes. *American Journal of Preventative Medicine*, 40(3): 362–76.

Emerald Works (2021) Welcome to Emerald Works. [online] Available at: https://emeraldworks.com (accessed 15 January 2022).

EUROPOL (2021) About Europol. [online] Available at: www.europol.europa.eu/about-europol (accessed 15 January 2022).

Facione, P A (1990) Critical Thinking: A Statement of Expert Consensus for Purposes of Educational Assessment and Instruction. *The Delphi Report*. American Philosophical Association, Doc No. ED 315423, pp 1–19.

Finn, W, McNeill, A and Mclean, F (2019) *Obtaining Initial Accounts from Victims and Witnesses: A Rapid Evidence Assessment to Support the Development of College Guidelines on Obtaining Initial Accounts from Victims and Witnesses*. [online] Available at: https://assets.college.police.uk/s3fs-public/2020-11/Initial_Accounts_REA.pdf (accessed 12 November 2021).

Francis, P (2018) Planning and Proposing Criminological Research. In Davis, P and Francis, P (eds) *Doing Criminological Research*. 3rd ed. Thousand Oaks, CA: Sage.

Georgetown University (2021) Evaluating Internet Resources. [online] Available at: www.library.georgetown.edu/tutorials/research-guides/evaluating-internet-content (accessed 15 January 2022).

Google (2021) *How to Search on Google*. [online] Available at: https://support.google.com/websearch/answer/134479?hl=en (accessed 15 January 2022).

Gov.uk (2020) Victims of Crime. [online] Available at: www.ethnicity-facts-figures.service.gov.uk/crime-justice-and-the-law/crime-and-reoffending/victims-of-crime/latest (accessed 15 January 2022).

Gov.uk (2021) How Government Works. [online] Available at: www.gov.uk/government/how-government-works#who-runs-government (accessed 8 March 2022).

Green, N (2008) Formulating and Refining a Research Question. In Gilbert, N (ed) *Researching Social Life*. 3rd ed. Los Angeles: Sage.

Greenstone, G (2010) The History of Bloodletting. *BC Medical Journal*, 52(1). [online] Available at: https://bcmj.org/premise/history-bloodletting (accessed 15 January 2022).

Gronmo, S (2020) *Social Research Methods: Qualitative, Quantitative and Mixed Methods Approaches*. 3rd ed. Thousand Oaks, CA: Sage.

Gudjonsson, G H (2003) *The Psychology of Interrogations and Confessions: A Handbook*. New York: John Wiley & Sons Ltd.

Hall, S (2018) Doing Ethnographic Research in Criminology. In Davies, P and Francis, P (eds) *Doing Criminological Research*. 3rd ed. Thousand Oaks, CA: Sage.

HM Government (2021) Mandatory Polygraph Tests Factsheet. [online] Available at: www.gov.uk/government/publications/domestic-abuse-bill-2020-factsheets/mandatory-polygraph-tests-factsheet (accessed 15 January 2022).

INTERPOL (2021) *What is INTERPOL?* Available at: www.interpol.int/en/Who-we-are/What-is-INTERPOL (accessed 15 January 2022).

Johnson, S D, Tilley, N and Bowers, K J (2015) Introducing EMMIE: An Evidence Rating Scale to Encourage Mixed-method Crime Prevention Synthesis Reviews. *Journal of Experimental Criminology*, 11: 459–73.

Jupp, V, Davies, P and Francis, P (2000) *Doing Criminological Research*. London; Thousand Oaks, CA: Sage.

Kahneman, D (2011) *Thinking Fast and Slow*. New York: Farra, Straus and Giroux.

Kime, S and Wheller, L (2018) The Policing Evaluation Toolkit. [online] Available at: https://whatworks.college.police.uk/Support/Pages/Evaluation-Toolkit.aspx (accessed 15 January 2022).

Laming, W H (2003) *The Victoria Climbié Inquiry*. CM5730. London: HMSO.

Leicester, M (2017) *Get a Better Grade: Seven Steps to Excellent Essays and Assignments*. 1st ed. Thousand Oaks, CA: Sage.

Lewandowski, D (2012) Credibility in Web Search Engines. In Folk, M and Apostel, S (eds) *Online Credibility and Digital Ethos: Evaluating Computer-Mediated Communication*. Hershey, PA: IGI Global.

Library of Congress (2021) FindLaw. [online] Available at: https://guides.loc.gov/free-case-law/findlaw (accessed 15 January 2022).

McConville, M and Hodgson, J (1993) *Custodial Legal Advice and the Right to Silence*. Research Study No. 16. The Royal Commission on Criminal Justice. London: HMSO.

McGurk, B J, Carr, M J and McGurk, D (1993) *Investigative Interviewing Courses for Police Officers: An Evaluation*. Police Research Series: Paper No. 4. London: Home Office Police Department.

Mews, A, Di Bella, L and Purver, M (2017) *Impact Evaluation of the Prison-based Core Sex Offender Treatment Programme*. London: Ministry of Justice.

Milne, R and Bull, R (1999) *Investigative Interviewing: Psychology and Practice*. Chichester: Wiley.

Ministry of Justice (2020) Criminal Procedure and Investigations Act 1996 (section 23 (1)) Code of Practice. [online] Available at: https://assets.publishing.service.gov.uk/government/uploads/system/uploads/attachment_data/file/931173/Criminal-procedure-and-investigations-act-1996.pdf (accessed 15 January 2022).

National Research Council (2003) *The Polygraph and Lie Detection*. Committee to review the scientific evidence on the polygraph. Washington, DC: The National Academies Press.

Neighbourhood Watch (2021) Our Research. [online] Available at: www.ourwatch.org.uk/our-research (accessed 15 January 2022).

ONS with Kantar Public (2015) Crime Survery for England & Wales. [online] Available at: www.crimesurvey.co.uk/en/index.html (accessed 25 February 2022).

Oxford Dictionaries (2013) Investigation. *Pocket Oxford English Dictionary.* Oxford: Oxford University Press.

Oxford English Dictionary (2013) Evidence. *Oxford English Dictionary*. Oxford: Oxford University Press.

Policing's National Collaboration Hub (2021) Knowledge Hub. [online] Available at: https://pds.police.uk/knowledge-hub/ (accessed 25 February 2022).

PRISMA (2021) Transparent Reporting of Systematic Reviews and Meta-Analyses. [online] Available at: www.prisma-statement.org (accessed 5 November 2021).

Ramiz, A, Rock, P and Strang, H (2020) Detecting Modern Slavery on Cannabis Farms: The Challenges of Evidence. *Cambridge Journal of Evidence-Based Policing*, 4: 202–17.

Richards, J (2010) *The Art and Science of Intelligence Analysis*. Oxford: Oxford University Press.

Roach, J, Cartwright, A, Weir, K, Richards, S and Weir, M (2020) Reducing Student Burglary Victimisation using the Nudge Approach. *Crime Prevention and Community Safety*, 22(4): 364–80.

Robinson, G (2018) Transforming Probation Services in Magistrates' Courts. *Probation Journal*, 65(3): 316–34.

Runciman, G (1993) *The Royal Commission on Criminal Justice* (Cmnd. 2263). London: HMSO.

RUSI (2021) Expertise. [online] Available at: https://rusi.org/expertise (accessed 15 January 2022).

Schein, E H (2010) *Organizational Culture and Leadership*. 4th ed. San Francisco, CA: Jossey Bass.

Search Engine Journal (2021) 17 Great Search Engines You Can Use Instead of Google. [online] Available at: www.searchenginejournal.com/alternative-search-engines/271409 (accessed 15 January 2022).

Sherman, L W (1998) *Evidence-Based Policing*. Ideas in American Policing Series. Washington, DC: Police Foundation. [online] Available at: www.policefoundation.org/wp-content/uploads/2015/06/Sherman-1998-Evidence-Based-Policing.pdf (accessed 15 January 2022).

Sherman, L W (2015) A Tipping Point for Totally Evidence Policing: Ten Ideas for Building an Evidence-based Police Agency. *Criminal Justice Review*, 25(1): 11–29.

Thelwall, M (2007) Extracting Accurate and Complete Results from Search Engines: Case Study Windows Live. *Journal of the American Society for Information Science and Technology*, 59(1): 38–50.

Transparency International UK (2016) *Empowering the UK to Recover Corrupt Assets: Unexplained Wealth Orders and Other New Approaches to Illicit Enrichment and Asset Recovery*. [online] Available at: www.transparency.org.uk/sites/default/files/pdf/publications/March2016_UWO.pdf (accessed 15 January 2022).

UKRI (2021) Who We Are. [online] Available at: www.ukri.org/about-us/who-we-are (accessed 15 January 2022).

United Nations (2011) *Handbook on Identity-related Crime*. [online] Available at: www.unodc.org/documents/treaties/UNCAC/Publications/Handbook_on_ID_Crime/10-57802_ebooke.pdf (accessed 15 January 2022).

United Nations Office on Drugs and Crime (UNODOC) (2021) Tools and Publications. [online] Available at: www.unodc.org/unodc/en/organized-crime/tools-and-publications. html (accessed 15 January 2022).

University College London (UCL) (2014) *Impact Case Study: Research Excellence Framework 3b*. [online] Available at: https://ref2014impact.azurewebsites.net/casestudies2/refserv ice.svc/GetCaseStudyPDF/40526 (accessed 15 January 2022).

Williamson, T M (1993) From Interrogation to Investigative Interviewing: Strategic Trends in Police Questioning. *Journal of Community and Applied Social Psychology*, 3: 89–99.

Wood, J L, Alleyne, E, Ciardhan, C Ó and Gannon, T A (2020) An Evaluation of Polygraph Testing by the Police to Manage Individuals Convicted or Suspected of Sexual Offending. [online] Available at: www.kent.ac.uk/school-of-psychology/downloads/kent_polygraph_ report.pdf (accessed 15 January 2022).

Yahoo (2021) UK.help.yahoo.com. [online] Available at: https://uk.search.yahoo.com/sea rch?p=how+to+search+on+yahoo&fr=yfp-search-sb (accessed 15 January 2022).

INDEX